A NEAR-RUN AFFAIR

New Zealanders in the battle for Crete, 1941

A NEAR-RUN AFFAIR

New Zealanders in the battle for Crete, 1941

Matthew Wright

REED

BY THE SAME AUTHOR:

Hawke's Bay — The History of a Province
Havelock North — The History of a Village
Napier — City of Style
Kiwi Air Power — The History of the RNZAF
Working Together — The History of Carter Oji Kokusaku Pan
Pacific Ltd 1971–1993
New Zealand's Engineering Heritage

Published by Reed Books, a division of Reed Publishing (NZ) Ltd,
39 Rawene Rd, Birkenhead, Auckland. Associated companies, branches
and representatives throughout the world. Website: www.reed.co.nz

© Matthew Wright 2000
The author asserts his moral rights in the work.

ISBN 0 7900 0732 0
First published 2000

Edited by Carolyn Lagahetau
Designed by Graeme Leather

Printed in New Zealand

CONTENTS

INTRODUCTION

History will show these campaigns in their true perspective.

— GENERAL SIR BERNARD FREYBERG, GENERAL OFFICER COMMANDING THE SECOND NEW ZEALAND DIVISION, REPORTING ON THE GREEK AND CRETE CAMPAIGNS TO THE MINISTER OF DEFENCE, FREDERICK JONES, 1941[1]

NEW ZEALAND soldiers arrived in Crete in early May 1941, short of equipment after a hasty evacuation from Greece. Three weeks later, the Germans attacked Crete from the air and sea. This first large-scale paratroop assault in history was risky, but by the next day the airfield at Maleme was in no-mans land, and efforts to retake it failed. The parachutists were backed by a powerful amphibious assault; there was no guarantee that this could be stopped by the Royal Navy, and for a while the fate of New Zealand's active armed force lay in the balance on an island half a world away from home.

This book takes a fresh look at the New Zealand experience on a remote Mediterranean island two generations ago. It is a 'how and why' history, a search for understanding and context, rather than an attempt to recount every event of a battle that also included British, Australian and Greek forces. Analysis is underpinned with a range of official documents, supported by the often poignant diaries and letters of participants — some written literally on the spot, as in the case of the soldier who, pinned down in a field by Stukas, was able to scribble down a few words about his experience while the marauding aircraft circled.

A number of people have given generously of their time and resources during my research for this book. I would particularly like to thank Jim Seymour, Mike Whatman and Trent Corbett, and General Freyberg's ADC's on Crete, Major Jack Griffiths MC and Sir John White MBE. I am also grateful to Sir John for his kind permission to make use of his photographic collection, and I extend my thanks to Windsor Jones of the Queen Elizabeth II Army Museum for his invaluable assistance with official photographs.

MATTHEW WRIGHT
August 2000

INTRODUCTION

GREEK OVERTURE

His Majesty's Government in New Zealand fully appreciates the necessity of making the most effective use of the comparatively limited military resources available in the Middle East . . . They cannot help feeling, nevertheless, that the task confronting an expedition of the size proposed is a most formidable and hazardous one.

— New Zealand Prime Minister Peter Fraser to the Secretary of State for Dominion Affairs, 26 February 1941[1]

The battle for Crete was the last act of the Balkan campaign that began in March 1941, when the Second New Zealand Expeditionary Force contributed to a meagre Anzac force intended to protect Greece from German assault.[2] Events were set in motion by the Italian dictator Benito Mussolini, who declared war on Greece in October 1940 after a series of embarrassing defeats at British hands in the African desert. Germany was not automatically involved, but the war created major complications in the volatile field of Balkan diplomacy — threatening the Ploesti oilfields, on which Germany relied — at a time when Hitler was looking to attack the Soviet Union.[3]

The move drew the British in on two counts. They were already at war with Italy, and they had guaranteed Greek neutrality in 1939. The latter provided both a de facto and an actual reason for intervention.[4] Although Britain did not have the resources to extend the conflict into a new theatre, the war opened up the prospect of mounting air strikes from Greek bases against the Ploesti oilfields, or directly against Italy. Plans were laid to forward-deploy aircraft into Greece, and to take islands in the Dodecanese for later use as air bases. Partly in response to the British, and partly because of heightened general tensions in the Balkans, Hitler felt obligated to secure his access to Romanian oil with 23 armoured divisions, which were deployed there in late 1940.[5] This was interpreted by the British as a threat, particularly as intercepted radio traffic revealed German plans to attack Greece and Turkey.[6] There were concerns that the assault might begin as early as January 1941.

Fearing that the Balkan states might fall one by one, British Prime Minister Winston

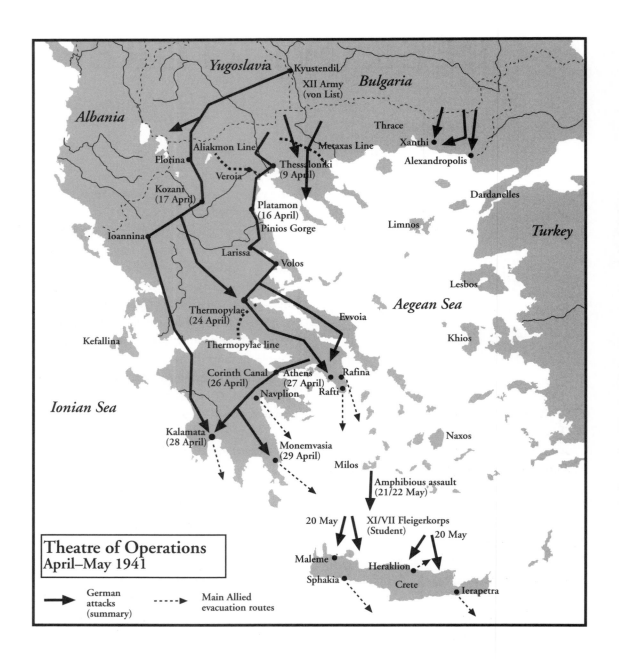

Theatre of Operations
April–May 1941

→ German attacks (summary)

┄┄► Main Allied evacuation routes

Churchill now planned to support the lead players directly, buying time for full British re-armament.[7] His Mediterranean advisers — Anthony Eden, General Sir John Dill, General Archibald Wavell and Admiral Sir Andrew Cunningham — favoured reinforcing Greece,[8] but in Churchill's mind the strategy relied on Turkish support. His 'very real hope' was that the Balkans would 'by our intervention be drawn to stand in the line together with . . . [Greece]'.[9] Not everybody agreed. While supporting in Greece, Wavell thought the intended German attack was part of a war of nerves intended to force the British away from Cyrenaica, though the 'mass of detail' did point to a likely German assault.[10] The Joint Chiefs of Staff in London were opposed on the basis that the Germans would take Greek intervention as a direct threat against Ploesti. Nor were there adequate forces; despite Wavell's stunning victories in Cyrenaica, reversal of fortune seemed likely in Africa as Rommel's campaign gained momentum. In January 1941, amid growing fears of a German attack into the Balkans, Churchill authorised the Greek strategy.[11] To make it work he needed Yugoslav and Turkish assistance, but he told Roosevelt's envoy Harry Hopkins that he was 'prepared for a setback'.[12]

It has been suggested that Churchill knew British intervention in Greece would probably provoke Hitler, and that the Greek strategy was a cynical manoeuvre intended to bring the Americans on side.[13] There is some basis to this argument; in December 1940, President Roosevelt certainly advised Churchill that opinion in the United States could be swayed by British military resurgence in Europe,[14] and Churchill also believed he could curry public opinion in France and Spain with a new campaign.[15] However, the British had guaranteed Greek security in April 1939, and by late 1940 the Balkan die had essentially been cast. Gaining public favour in America was merely a bonus,[16] although Roosevelt later categorised this 'heroic' work in Greece as 'very useful'.[17]

The Greeks were less enthusiastic. Dictator John Metaxas feared that extensive British forces in Greece would provoke the Germans, but he died at the end of January. His successor Alexander Koryzis was more open to persuasion, although the Greeks never did turn to Britain 'for succour' as Churchill claimed to the House in April.[18] Hitler's response was as Metaxas had feared. He exerted massive diplomatic pressure on Yugoslavia and Bulgaria, and the latter joined the Axis powers at the beginning of March. The Panzers rolled over the Danube on 2 March, heading for the Greek and Yugoslav borders.

Churchill began to entertain doubts about the operation around this time. Only three divisions — two Australian and one New Zealand — plus a British armoured brigade, could be spared. Support from

New Zealanders leaving Egypt for an 'unknown destination', which was in fact Greece and Operation LUSTRE, March 1941.

Sir John White Collection

Turkey seemed unlikely, and Churchill now felt that defeat for British forces in Greece would have a worse moral effect than fighting the campaign in the first place.[19] But the Germans were already in Bulgaria, and Sir Michael Palairet — the British ambassador in Athens — objected to any breach of Britain's commitment.[20] The arrival of British forces under the overall command of Lieutenant-General Sir Henry Wilson prompted dissent within the Greek leadership, including discussion of an army-led revolt to avert the expected German response, but nothing was done.

The British did not anticipate problems getting the go-ahead to send Kiwi troops into Greece. Although New Zealand had been a self-governing Dominion since 1907, the government still looked on Britain as mentor, guide and master. The Labour administration that came to power in 1935 was more independently minded than its predecessors, but when it came to the crunch Prime Minister Peter Fraser and his cabinet still had great difficulty refusing British requests. This attitude hardened only slowly.[21]

British overtures were frank. Viscount Cranborne, Secretary of State for Dominion Affairs, asked the New Zealand government for authority to deploy the Second New Zealand Division to Greece in late February. Failure to help Greece, he argued, would 'have a grave effect on public opinion . . . particularly in the United States . . .'[22] Fraser concurred on the understanding that the New Zealand division would be accompanied by an armoured brigade, but when he learned of deployments in more detail at the end of February he had second thoughts. The task was 'a most formidable and hazardous one', and he wanted confirmation that 'the force is in fact adequate to meet the probable scale of attack'.[23] The British response emphasised heavy reliance on the Turks and hinted at a Yugoslav alliance.[24] Matters were complicated by a decision to postpone an invasion of Rhodes and several islands in the Dodecanese, which would have given the British air bases within range of the Greek mainland.

In early March Cranborne despatched six telegrams to New Zealand to show 'how the matter has been thrashed out',[25] and asked for formal consent. It took two days to decipher this material in Wellington. The documents included a gloomy telegram from Churchill to Anthony Eden, to the effect that British intervention in Greece would fail without 'most improbable' Turkish or Yugoslav help.[26] There was also a very despondent analysis by the British Chiefs of Staff, with which the New Zealand cabinet generally agreed.

Fraser's response pushed the mindset of his day.[27] He told Churchill the operation was 'obviously much more hazardous than that previously contemplated', and urged 'most careful attention' to the 'strongest possible' sea and air escort for the transports, along with 'full and immediate consideration of the means of withdrawal both on land and at sea'. He could give approval only if the 'full British force contemplated can clearly be made available at the appropriate time'.[28] Churchill promised Fraser 'faithful, unremitting endeavour [to] make good the request and assumption'.[29] Two days later Cranborne forwarded an assessment by the Chiefs of Staff which put the plan in a more favourable light.[30]

On 25 March the Croatian-dominated Yugoslav government threw in its lot with the Germans, but a revolt next day replaced the government with a pro-Allied Serbian military authority. In response, Hitler demanded the destruction of Yugoslavia.[31] On 6 April the XII Army under General von List simultaneously entered Yugoslavia and Greece. Forces committed to the Greek front included five Panzer divisions, three mountain divisions, and two motorised and eight infantry divisions of the regular Wehrmacht, supported by an SS division. It was an overwhelming force.

Operation LUSTRE: the Greek campaign

*The Huns advanced slowly and when they got
their guns up they began to tickle our boys and
we were lucky not to be shelled where we were.*

— J.N. MACLEAN, 22ND NEW ZEALAND BATTALION,
2NZEF, GREECE, 1941[32]

RIGHT: **On the way to Greece — General Bernard Freyberg with Captain Portal of HMS *York*.**

Sir John White Collection

BELOW: **HMS *Gloucester* and *Bonaventure* from the bridge of HMS *York* — part of the convoy taking the first New Zealand advance parties to Greece, March 1941.**

Sir John White Collection

While some of the New Zealand troops who crossed to Greece during early March anxiously anticipated combat, others looked forward to playing tourist in another new and strange land — one made stranger by the fact that war between Greece and Germany did not break out until after the first Kiwis arrived, and German military attachés shadowed the troops for a few days without hindrance. 'Wonderful city, Athens & wonderful people,' Harold Loftus scribbled in his pocket diary.[33] J.N. Maclean, leading an anti-aircraft (AA) crew attached to the headquarters unit of 25 Battalion, found the early Greek experience enlightening. 'They have a very good beer in Greece and also excellent cheap wines and a real fine drink called Konlak,' he wrote to his parents.

The New Zealand Division was led by Major General Bernard Freyberg.[34] Freyberg, who was considered 'brave as a lion',[35] had joined the Royal Naval Division in 1914, won the DSO at Gallipoli and the VC on the Western Front,[36] and had been repeatedly wounded in action. His friend Winston Churchill once counted '27 separate scars and gashes' on Freyberg's body.[37] He was an outstanding tactician and strategist whose leadership was summed up by Field Marshal Bernard Montgomery as having 'rarely been seen in the history of the British Army'.[38] Despite revisionist efforts to 'demythologise' both the New Zealand soldiers and Freyberg as a commander,[39] this observation remains apt; in many ways, historians have overcompensated for the myth.

Freyberg also took due account of the desire of the New Zealand government to look after the men — Prime Minister Peter Fraser and his cabinet had no intention of seeing New Zealand bled white in a second Western Front or Gallipoli. Freyberg had a genuine 'feel' for the men he led — demonstrated in just one way by his desire

RIGHT: **New Zealand troops disembark at Piraeus, Athens, March 1941.**
Sir John White Collection

BELOW: **Two New Zealand provosts in Athens during the early part of the Greek campaign.**
Sir John White Collection

during the Crete campaign to have full details of what was coming passed down to them.[40] Fraser met Freyberg in London after the general was appointed to command the 2NZEF in November 1939, and was:

. . . at once struck not only by his personality and by his obvious experience and confidence, but particularly by the supreme importance which he clearly attached to the proper treatment of the troops and to the necessity of proper and timely administrative measures to ensure their welfare and safety . . . [Freyberg] invariably took care of his men even at the risk of his own safety.[41]

Jack Griffiths, Freyberg's ADC, recalled that the general was a 'wonderful man, and we were so lucky to have his services throughout the war'.[42] Freyberg was, in turn, very proud of his men. Divisional training in Egypt gave him a healthy appreciation of Kiwi spirit, and before they left for Greece he told them: 'I have never seen troops that impressed me more . . . you must steel yourselves to overcome the ordeal of the modern battlefield . . . The honour of the New Zealand division is in your keeping. It could not be in better hands.'[43] This was not mere morale-boosting propaganda. Privately he wrote:

I am back with the Nzers [sic] after twenty six years absence. I find in them qualities of heart and mind that in my youth were not apparent to my unskilled eye. I believe that there is a higher standard of talent and character in the ranks of the men of the New Zealand division than any troops I have seen.[44]

He had the highest hopes for the campaign to come, writing that he had been in both of Churchill's previous 'military adventures', and hoping that the third 'will, I trust, be the one which will redeem the others. I know that my troops will do well.'[45]

The Kiwis were joined in Greece by 6 Australian Division under Major General Mackey, the whole forming 2 Anzac Corps under Lieutenant General Sir Thomas Blamey. Freyberg thought Blamey's experience 'and the Australian's fighting qualities' would 'prove great assets'.[46] They came under the overall command of Lieutenant General Sir Henry Wilson. The odds, however, seemed stacked against the allies. The Greeks were able to promise only sixteen battalions, and the Germans had — in Fraser's words — 'almost unlimited' strength.[47] The German advance through Yugoslavia threatened a flank attack, and a fresh campaign by the Afrika Korps in Cyrenaica meant the second Australian division had to be held in Africa. Churchill apologised for breaking the promises on which the New Zealanders had been deployed, but was sure the government would 'appreciate the overriding factors which have since intervened'.[48] This did not help the position in Greece. Even when a decision was taken to dig in at Aliakmon, north of Mount Olympus, the general feeling was that it would be May before the Anzacs could resist the expected attack. Freyberg did not like it, drafting a letter to Fraser warning that the plan was 'ill conceived' and 'violates every principle of military strategy'.[49] This draft was not apparently sent, because Fraser was surprised to learn of Freyberg's reservations about Greece when they met in early June.[50]

Coal shortages halted trains after 15 March and the troops took to the road. 25 Battalion spent three days on the move, at first on a 'good bitumen road . . . with plenty of room for the traffic to pass', but ultimately over 'nothing more than a cart track wandering over the hills'.[51] Peasant girls threw flowers, and 'when we went through a village the population would turn out en masse and there was a cheering welcome which was very nice'.[52] By early April the entire division was digging in. J.N. Maclean had 'quite a good time . . . for about 2½ weeks', and for five days camped with his gun crew on a riverbank:

We started out soon after breakfast each morning, and went back to a convenient spot we had picked near the river. It was very like the Tukituki [River] and we used to take our rations and a billy, and managed to make ourselves very comfortable. We would set up the gun and then swim and sunbathe and do

all our washing of clothes in the river. It was beautifully fine and quite hot so we thoroughly enjoyed it. The town was only about a mile away so we used to go through there if we wanted to buy anything.[53]

Elsewhere it was colder, and for some the change of climate came as a shock. J.E.J. Westbrook recalled that 18 Battalion 'felt the cold pretty bad when we first arrived and within a short time of leaving Egypt had our first experience of snow'.[54] James Pickett was shocked by abysmal Easter weather. 'Good Friday in the pass,' he scribbled in his pocket diary, 'cold — rain — wind.' Hail

For most of the New Zealanders and their commanders, Greece was unfamiliar territory. Here, General Freyberg (at left) and his officers survey the lie of the land around Mount Olympus.

Sir John White Collection

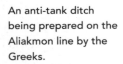

An anti-tank ditch
being prepared on the
Aliakmon line by the
Greeks.

Sir John White Collection

followed next day, and Easter Sunday was freezing. 'Snow *cold*.'[55]

The first encounters between New Zealanders and Germans came on 10 April. A 'great splash of smoke told us the last bridge had gone,' Brigadier James Hargest wrote later to his wife, 'and I was in the front line.'[56] The blitzkrieg was spearheaded by the Junkers Ju 87 dive-bomber, giving the men a taste of the conditions that underpinned the Crete campaign. 'With the plane's engines and screamers, bomb screamers and bursting planes and defenders' machine guns you can't exactly hear a pin drop,' J.N. Maclean wrote. He saw some spectacular dive-bombing and despite being in charge of an anti-aircraft gun felt 'very helpless' under seventy or eighty German aircraft circling overhead. He opened fire on a German aircraft and 'felt a

great thrill as the tracer curved towards him, the first shot of the war which I fired'. The aircraft 'carried on quite calmly and disappeared around the hill'.[57]

Although the initial attacks were repulsed, the outcome was inevitable. A German fuelling halt gave time for Wilson to organise a fighting withdrawal, and by the time the Germans were on the move again the allies had pulled back to Mount Olympus, where the New Zealand 21 Battalion fought a delaying action. These manoeuvres cost the Wehrmacht heavily — in one action the Kiwis captured nearly 150 Germans. Westbrook was impressed by the thoroughness with which the Germans equipped their troops, 'every man having a revolver and a superb pair of binoculars'.[58] He later found 'a lot of the boys . . . sporting German field glasses and revolvers'.[59]

Unfortunately the Greek Central Macedonian Army did not pull back in good order, and Commander in Chief General Papagos suggested the British should pull out. Churchill agreed, promising Fraser that 'the gallant New Zealand troops' would be 'evacuated successfully with as much of their equipment as can be carried away'.[60] To hold the Germans for long enough, Wilson proposed a 'short and strong' line running from Thermopylae to Euboea.[61] This required a retreat under air attack along muddy roads, coalescing on the plains of Thessaly. It also meant abandoning the Greeks. Maclean felt 'rotten' about leaving the villagers, 'especially when they have [given] us such a kind farewell'. To Maclean the drive to Larissa was:

. . . the worst time we had during the whole show. The road was packed with trucks and as we reached Larissa the fun started. The town is fairly large and the Jerrys were raiding it nearly all the time. It is a terrible sight to go into a deserted, wrecked and burning town.[62]

South of the town the Kiwis came under constant air attack. Stukas 'came at us all the time-dive bombing and machine gunning, sometimes only 50 feet up'. Casualties were low, although the Germans 'got a lot of trucks'. Maclean AA gun was attacked by an Me-110. 'It was a close shave and when it was over I began to feel afraid.' By dark the men were 'all very exhausted and strained,

TOP: **Three of the Allied commanders (from left to right): General Thomas Blamey, commander ANZAC Corps: General Sir Henry Maitland Wilson, overall Commander in Chief of LUSTRE force; and General Bernard Freyberg of the New Zealand Division.**
Sir John White Collection

BOTTOM: **General Freyberg (right) and 5 Brigade commander Brigadier James Hargest visiting the New Zealand infantry rearguard position at Thermopylae during the withdrawal.**
Sir John White Collection

but very relieved that the daylight had gone and we were safe'.[63] Westbrook thought:

. . . if it wasn't for their air force we could hold them, but there is no denying that the Luftwaffe is colossal. We were bombed and machine gunned by thirty Heinkel dive bombers and twelve Messerschmitt fighters one day then were visited the following day by thirty Junkers dive bombers. The din was Bedlam itself but the damage was nil, but even so it gets a bit nerve racking.[64]

Freyberg's headquarters convoy was hit, 'about 12 miles south of Larissa . . . [where] we had 4 vehicles knocked out in one dive bombing attack & 5 more in another attack a few minutes later'.[65] The Germans reached Larissa on 19 April. By next day the Anzacs

were establishing positions on the Thermopylae line, but were still heavily engaged and under almost constant air attack. Lieutenant Colonel William Gentry later wrote that the Germans — once established in the Larissa airfield — were:

. . . close enough for their fighters to operate & the Messerschmitts had great fun up & down the roads with their little cannon guns. We went out from there with the intention of going off from the beaches around Athens, but only Hargest's brigade managed to do that. The others went off to go to the southern part of Greece, the Peloponnese . . .[66]

On 21 April the British War Cabinet ordered the Royal Navy to take the men off.

Evacuation to Crete

The New Zealand government learned of the desperate turn of events on 22 April, when the Australian government warned that their latest report from Blamey was 'most alarming'.

In view of the seriousness of the position . . . regarding the shortage of arms, the inadequacy of fighting equipment, and the heavy reduction of Air Force strength, evacuation of our troops will now be rendered doubly hazardous and it is feared that if extreme pressures are not taken it will end in a catastrophe . . . Blamey's message is so alarming that we ask you to give it your utmost exclusive attention.[67]

Fraser took up the case and demanded 'a safe and rapid evacuation from Greece'.[68] He was fobbed off by Churchill, who had no doubt that the 'early re-embarkation' of the Anzac troops would be necessary, but although this would get 'precedence over any other consideration except that of honour', the battle in Libya could not 'be endangered by withdrawing too much of our Air Force from there'.[69] A few days later he told Admiral Sir Andrew Cunningham, Commander in Chief of the Mediterranean Fleet, that the 'prime responsibility' of the Mediterranean fleet was to 'sever all communications betwen Italy and Africa'. Cunningham accepted the order but felt there were 'two other commitments of

LEFT: **During the period of the rearguard actions Freyberg travelled by car, daily visiting the three brigades in action. During this period his cars came under attack from strafing aircraft. This photograph shows Freyberg, his driver and staff just south of Larissa, surveying damage done to one of his cars.**
Sir John White Collection

RIGHT: **Some of Freyberg's staff after the strafing.**
Sir John White Collection

Greek soldiers pulling back at dawn, on the road during withdrawal south of Athens.

Sir John White Collection

General Freyberg (right) with a Greek priest during the withdrawal to the Peloponnese.

Sir John White Collection

immediate importance' — one of them taking the army off Greece.[70]

Actually executing the withdrawal was another matter; the Luftwaffe dominated coastal waters around Greece and evacuation from the harbours was almost impossible. Harold Loftus discovered this the hard way when he 'left [the] benzine guard station in trucks for a port 130 miles north & west of Athens'. He was disappointed. 'Place was bombed,' he wrote

in his diary. 'Also boats . . . bombed & machine gunned heavily all day. Not one of our planes has come to help us.'[71] Most of the equipment had to be destroyed, 'much to our regret,' according to George Craigie of the 6th Field Regiment, 'as most of our vehicles had only done about 2000 miles — just run in.'[72]

By 26 April the only New Zealand unit north of the Corinth Canal was 4 Brigade, which with Australian Royal Artillery and Royal Engineers covered the 'withdrawal to the Peleponnese for final evacuation'.[73] The Germans made a surprise parachute raid to capture the bridge over the Corinth Canal, which failed when New Zealand sappers blew it up,[74] but a number were captured, including Frank Renouf.[75] By this time the men were 'getting dirtier and sleepy and bad food and nervy'.[76] Westbook's unit abandoned their trucks and walked 'eight or nine miles' to the beach:

A lot of the gear was intact but we saw the

On the road to Monemvasia, looking back to the final rearguard position taken by 6 Brigade, late on the day of the evacuation to Crete.

Sir John White Collection

Greeks helping themselves to it before we left so probably the Huns didn't get so much. Most of the trucks were ruined by the simple method of draining out the oil and setting the motor going. We put sugar in the benzine of our truck just to help things along.[77]

The slog to the coast was something he hoped 'never [to] go through again'. Gentry later wrote to his wife that the New Zealand commanders were 'very worried about old Putt [Puttick] . . . but fortunately we were able to get in touch with him by wireless'. He tried to keep his account fairly light-hearted, explaining that Puttick:

. . . had a fairly close shave, but managed to get off from the beaches east of Athens. Rusty Page's Bn had a little battle with the parachutists & the next day we went back to the vicinity of Tripolis. After that we did a long move to the east coast near the tip of Greece to . . . Monemvasia. It was done by night & we were able to get good lying up areas under trees where the Air Force failed to spot us . . . We embarked by night & it was almost like a peace time move . . . I must say that the Navy did a great job of work.[78]

By 28 April Loftus and his unit were 'in a great orange grove', and he jotted down a few thoughts in his pocket diary as they hid from the Luftwaffe:

Wrong place really as it is a great target for the cursed Huns that speed past & bomb all the time . . . Well here we are & I'm not down in the dumps, but sorry we haven't done much, unless we enticed the Hun down into Greece to give the other fronts a chance to trap them. I hope that is what has happened. I hear Turkey is in but it may be only a rumour . . . What a great pity to have death sailing around in such a beautiful country. This curse surely can't go on. I hear the Hun planes coming again so must get down flat.[79]

Freyberg inherited command on Wilson's departure, and discovered that the British had issued cash for their troops to buy food and hire boats if they were left behind. He promptly distributed £2000 to the New Zealanders for the same purpose.[80] Although ordered to return to Egypt, he explained that he was in the middle of fighting a battle, and in the event was one of the last to leave Monemvasia in the early hours of 29 April.[81]

Despite the risks, Cunningham did not hesitate to commit the Mediterranean Fleet to the evacuation. Seven ships were lost in 'Operation Demon', but 50,662 troops were evacuated.[82] The exhausted men were told to 'dump nearly everything' — the direct order was to leave all but personal arms.

Top: **Two Australians and two New Zealanders on board HMS** *Ajax* **after leaving Greece.**

Sir John White Collection

Bottom: **Troops evacuated from Greece relax on board HMS** *Ajax.*

Sir John White Collection

Hargest was not enthusiastic and 'went to the GOC (not ours of course) and told him on no account would I give up my arms & he agreed'.[83] He also persuaded Captain Petrie of the HMS *Calcutta* to take men 'long after the agreed-upon time'.[84] Other units were not so fortunate. Maclean saved only his 'toilet gear and 2 pairs of sox [sic] and one or two personal things'. Westbrook's experience was typical:

. . . when we climbed aboard at 2 o'clock in the morning they gave us every assistance, a cheery word, a smile and a pat on the back. Hot soup, cocoa and tea were waiting for us and cigarettes were being handed round. We were packed in like sardines and there were many soldiers who were jammed in corners and couldn't get out for refreshments, and there were many who preferred to flop down and sleep rather than bother about something to drink.[85]

Among the soldiers were two Greek women who boarded a destroyer disguised as Australians — the ruse was discovered when 'the girls became distressed' by the heat below decks 'and reacted . . . by shedding their Aussie uniforms'.[86] Out of 16,720 New Zealanders in Greece, 7100 were evacuated to Crete, 1300 went first to Crete and then Egypt, and 6054 went direct to Egypt. This left 2266 New Zealanders back in Greece, some 13.6 percent of the force and 19.1 percent of total Allied losses.[87]

THE ATTACK ON CRETE
1–19 MAY 1941

The first objective will most certainly be the three aerodromes Heraklion, Retimo and Maleme . . . if the aerodromes hold out, as they will, the whole [German] plan will fail . . . Although this appreciation has not mentioned sea landings on beaches, the possibility of these attacks must not be overlooked; but they will be of secondary importance to those from the air.

— Brigadier General Staff, 'Appreciation —
German Plan for attack on Crete,' 12 May 1941[1]

The British had decided to 'aid and maintain the defence of Crete to the utmost'[2] as early as 17 April. Although ostensibly this was to shore up the Greek government — which evacuated to the island on 22 April — it was actually to address British interests. Loss of the island would affect the British ability to maintain a blockade against the Italian fleet, and to support Malta — long seen as a linchpin of the Mediterranean theatre.

Efforts to bolster the defences began when war broke out between Greece and Italy, however plans to garrison the island to

divisional strength came to nothing and only an infantry battalion was deployed, along with 63 anti-aircraft guns and one radar unit. The guns were divided between Suda, Maleme and Heraklion, and 10,000 rifles were distributed to locals. A scheme to establish five new airfields was held up by inter-service argument. A Marine Naval Base Defence Organisation was ordered to the island in March, to improve the

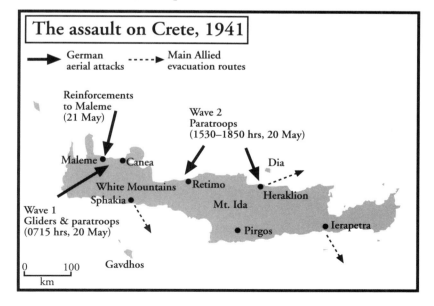

The assault on Crete, 1941

→ German aerial attacks   ⇢ Main Allied evacuation routes

Reinforcements to Maleme (21 May)
Wave 2 Paratroops (1530–1850 hrs, 20 May)
Maleme
Canea
Dia
White Mountains
Retimo
Heraklion
Sphakia
Mt. Ida
Wave 1 Gliders & paratroops (0715 hrs, 20 May)
Pirgos
Ierapetra
Gavdhos
0   100
km

ABOVE: **HMS *Ajax* in Suda Bay after bringing troops to Crete from Greece.**
Sir John White Collection

RIGHT: **To the New Zealanders Crete was a land of bare soil, olive groves and rugged hills.**
Sir John White Collection

defences of Suda Bay naval base, though much of it did not arrive until May.

Freyberg arrived intending to pass through, but was instead made overall commander of CREFORCE on 30 April. The 4th and 5th New Zealand Infantry brigades, including 28 (Maori) Battalion, and 'large parties of artillery, army service corps, engineers, cavalry and machine gunners'

were dumped on Crete.[3] Equipment was short. Control of the two New Zealand brigades on the island went to Puttick.

Freyberg advised New Zealand Minister of Defence Frederick Jones about the government money he had distributed during the last days of evacuation from Greece, adding that he had 'offered to pay any Greek shipowner . . . for any New Zealand soldier . . . rescued from mainland or island', and asking for financial authority to do so.[4] Walter Nash — acting Prime Minister, as Fraser had departed for Cairo — lost no time in assuring Freyberg that 'full approval' had been given 'to all the sums disposed of by you in the manner stated'. Furthermore, he was 'authorised to expend any further sums you consider necessary to assist the rescue of New Zealanders from Greece'.[5]

Men continued to arrive from Greece during May, mostly on small boats. Harold Loftus and a small group rowed for three days before being forced back to Greece. Hiding from the Germans and desperate for food, they finally found passage in a small boat on 11 May, arriving on Crete three days later.[6] George Craigie reached Crete with another group of soldiers on board a 40-foot sailing boat, 'once a small coal cargo tub'. They weathered several storms before 'a great breeze took us in to a very rocky coastline'.[7]

For a few days the evacuated Anzac troops found peace amid the olive groves and

THE ATTACK ON CRETE

For a few glorious days in early May, the New Zealanders rescued from the Greek campaign had time to relax, swim and sunbathe on Crete. Here, Kiwis enjoy the beach near Canea.

DA11024 Kippenberger Military Archive & Research Library, Army Museum, Waiouru

fields of Crete. They swam, sunbathed, rested and ate, and were welcomed with open arms by the Cretans. But the soldiers needed more than good health. They were desperately short of everything from weapons to eating utensils. War artist Peter McIntyre found that most of the men only had the clothes they stood up in.[8] J.E.J. Westbrook was one of the lucky ones. He had 'hung on to all I could' during the evacuation from Greece and was 'one of the few that doesn't have to use a tin for mug and plate. Three of us share my fork and spoon.'[9]

'Informal' swimming attire was common in most theatres of war and attracted no unusual attention.

1990.1756 Kippenberger Military Archive & Research Library, Army Museum, Waiouru

Einsatz MERKUR and ULTRA intelligence

An attack on Crete was first discussed by the Germans in early April, during 'several conferences between the Chief of General Staff, the Chief of Staff of Luftflotte 4, the Chief of Staff Fleigerkorps XI and the Commander of Fleiger Division XII'.[10] Luftwaffe commander Hermann Goering was enthusiastic when approached on 15 April, but Hitler viewed the Balkan campaign as a diversion and rejected the proposal. Generaloberst Kurt Student, Commander in Chief of Fleigerkorps XI, then persuaded Goering to facilitate a further meeting with Hitler on 21 April. With the support of the ebullient Reichsmarschall, Student was able to convince Hitler to authorise the plan, which became Directive No. 28, Einsatz MERKUR (Operation Mercury).

In 1925, Hitler had dismissed New Zealanders as tree dwellers who 'climb around on all fours',[11] but his commanders regarded the Anzacs as formidable opponents.[12] Despite the impending assault on the Soviet Union, Student was given the 5th Mountain Division to support Fleigerkorps XI — some 22,750 men in total. Air transport was provided by 493 Junkers Ju 52/3m transports and 80 DFS 230 gliders. Elements of Fleigerkorps VIII under General von Richthofen — a relative of the First World War ace — provided air support.

Each force had different ideas about how the attack might be mounted. Luftflotte 4 command favoured occupying western Crete and driving east, but Fleigerkorps XI commanders — under Student — identified seven points requiring simultaneous assault, including Maleme, Retimo and Candia. In the end the Luftwaffe High Command required attacks on 'the four most important points at intervals, so as to enable [Richthofen's] Fleigerkorps VIII to provide the maximum protection'.[13] The final plan, which developed from these initial concepts, relied on surprise, excellent training, and a good deal of luck.

Mounting the assault was not easy. There were not enough transports to move the required force simultaneously against four targets; a first wave was to take Maleme and Canea in the morning. By afternoon the

German soldiers parading through Athens after the end of the Greek campaign. This photograph was found in a German camera captured by New Zealand soldiers during the campaign, and subsequently widely reproduced.

Jim Seymour Collection

Adolf Hitler and Hermann Goering (both arrowed on the original print) visited their troops in Athens before the assault on Crete began. The informality of this particular meeting, snapped by a soldier standing on a nearby truck, was characteristic of Hitler's behaviour around his beloved troops.

1991.1516 Kippenberger Military Archive & Research Library, Army Museum, Waiouru

transports would return to drop a second wave over Retimo and Heraklion. Seaborne units would follow up the initial lodgements made from the air. The plan relied on reaching the first objectives within 24 hours. It was risky — and made more so by the fact that the Germans grossly underestimated the number of Allied troops on the island.[14] The XI Air Corps official war diarist noted that 'utmost difficulty was encountered' obtaining the necessary forces and supplies, which 'had to be overcome in the shortest possible time and with very limited means' requiring 'improvisations of all kinds'.[15] The 'most vulnerable' bottleneck was petrol and oil:

Since medium Pol supply columns were not available, the entire supply was carried out from barrels. The number of barrels which had been obtained with great trouble, finally only just sufficed for two sorties. As it was essential, at the opening of the attack, to have ready on the airfields supplies for 3 sorties, continuous return of the empty barrels to Piraeus and their rapid refilling had to be ensured. A completely inadequate filling installation in Piraeus made the carrying through of this supply a matter of the greatest difficulty. Altogether, during the period 17 to 20.5, 3.6 million litres of fuel, equal to 3 sorties for 10 Ju groups, had to be brought up to the airfield by these primitive means.[16]

It took nearly three weeks to bring the troops into the Peloponnese — partly against the flow of traffic as the Wehrmacht redeployed for the assault on the Soviet Union. By this time ten airfields had been prepared around Athens, and most of the DFS 230B-1 gliders had arrived from Germany. The biggest bottleneck remained aircraft. The Ju 52s had been heavily worked during the Greek campaign and had to be flown to bases in Germany, Austria and Czechoslovakia for overhaul. By 15 May — when Student originally hoped to mount the attack — nearly 500 were back in Greece 'thanks to the ceaseless efforts of workshops in the Reich and the co-operation of the Chief of Works Department',[17] but fuel remained a problem, and the assault had to be delayed first to 18 and then 20 May. The XII Air Corps war diarist recorded that the ships,

much delayed by enemy submarine and mining activities, only began to arrive from 17.5.41 onwards . . . The unloading of the cargoes in the extensively damaged harbour installations with the assistance of German Mountain troops and Greek labour, and their transportation by means of MT columns, improvised from unit vehicles, along a few, heavily used roads, could only be managed by overcoming considerable friction . . . General HQ XII Air Corps did not have at its disposal a supply organisation suitable for the solution of tasks of this kind. Everything had to be improvised. Some easing . . . was achieved by

placing the Senior Column commander of Air Fleet under general HQ XI Air Corps.[18]

Encrypted German radio traffic carrying details of the plan as it developed was intercepted by a British listening post at Abbassia and decoded by the electro-mechanical COLOSSUS computer at Bletchley Park. This ability to crack German encryption in useful time was known as ULTRA, and it was one of the most closely guarded secrets of the war. Indeed, it was considered so valuable that field commanders were usually not given information obtained solely from that source because of the risk of compromise. ULTRA information was also utilised with no explanation other than that it was to be regarded as a reliable source, and the hint that it came from highly placed spies.[19] This complicated Freyberg's defence of his actions later; he could not reveal ULTRA-related rationales either during the official investigation in June, or in the post-war years when controversy raged.

The Germans preparing for the attack on Crete never suspected their various codes had been broken, though they knew there was a leak somewhere, bitterly complaining that the 'deployment of the Parachute troops and the Ju groups in the Athens area, the loading and clearing of ships, were known to the enemy intelligence service in every detail'. They put it down to 'British soldiers in civilian clothes, perhaps also American consular officials . . . at the disposal of the enemy for the collection of information on an extensive scale'. What puzzled them was lack of corroborating evidence. 'Offences against security on the German side have not been discovered,' the author of the XI Air Corps war diary noted drily.[20]

The British had the initial German plan by 27 April, from ULTRA sources but syphoned to the Middle East via a Joint Intelligence Committee report entitled 'Scale of Attack on Crete', JIC (41) 181.[21] A summary, preserved in the GOC NZEF file, was available in Crete by 29 April. In its clipped militarese it warned that:

German attack Crete by simultaneous air borne [sic] reinforcements from seaborne expeditions believed imminent. Scale airborne attack estimated 3000/4000 parachutists or airborne troops in first sortie. 2 or 3 sorties per day possible from Greece and 3 or 4 from Rhodes if Rhodes not used as DIVE bombers base . . . Estimated both troops and shipping ample for seaborne operations and lighters for transport tanks also believed available hence scale seaborne attack dependent on extent to which enemy can evade our naval force.[22]

On 30 April, Wavell convened a meeting in Crete with selected officers, including Freyberg, at which the options were discussed in light of this intelligence. They had already decided to hold the island, and now turned to the practicalities.[23] Although a seaborne assault was expected, most of the officers had no doubt about the primacy of air attack, as the notes on the conference reveal:

Scale of attack given at 5–6000 airborne tps. [Scale of] Naval attack not known . . . Enemy objectives — HERAKLION and MALEME aerodromes . . . No additional air support will be forthcoming . . . The object was defined to deny the enemy the use of CRETE as an Air Base.[24]

The only dissenter was Major General Weston, who 'pointed out that a sea borne attack was very probable and that as far as he could see, the Navy would not be able to do much about it'. Freyberg was given

CREFORCE HQ was established in a quarry on the eastern high ground above Canea, with a panoramic view from Maleme to Canea. This elderly Cretan was a mason working on the headquarters' buildings.

Sir John White Collection

command of CREFORCE at this meeting. He protested the appointment, indicating that the New Zealand government would not agree to splitting the division, but Wavell insisted. Although Freyberg was 'most anxious to get all our men back to base and again re-constitute the Division',[25] he accepted the inevitable and 'commenced to make himself familiar with the situation', something 'not made any easier by the move of Force HQ from CANEA to inadequate dugouts in the foothills to the east of the town'.[26]

Freyberg advised Fraser on 1 May that the 'decision has been taken in London that Crete must be held at all cost'. He passed on a summary of the 29 April intelligence with the comment that 'in my opinion Crete can only be held with the full support of the Navy and Air Force', there was 'no evidence of naval forces capable of guaranteeing us against seaborne invasion, and the air force in the island consists of six Hurricanes and seventeen obsolete aircraft'. This matched the opinions already aired at the conference the previous day. The combined assault prompted Freyberg to warn Fraser of the 'grave situation in which the bulk of the Division is placed' and to recommend 'that you bring pressure to bear on the highest plane in London either to supply us with sufficient means to defend the island, or to review the decision that Crete must be held'.[27] After making this protest, Freyberg then 'set about making the island as secure

as the limited time and materials at my disposal allowed'.[28]

These limits were severe. Although Freyberg had around 40,000 troops of several nationalities on the island, about 10,000 of these were without arms, and 'with little or no employment other than getting into trouble'.[29] They were insufficient to 'oppose the enemy at every place where he might land'.[30] On 1 May, Freyberg advised Wavell that his forces were 'totally inadequate to meet the attack envisaged', continuing:

Unless the number of fighter aircraft is greatly increased and naval forces made available to deal with a seaborne attack I cannot hope to hold out with land forces alone, which as a result of the campaign in Greece, are now devoid of any artillery, have insufficient tools for digging, very little transport, and inadequate war reserves of equipment and ammunition. The force here can and will fight, but cannot hope to repel invasion without full support from the Navy and Air Force. If, for other reasons, these cannot be made available at once, I urge that the question of holding Crete should be reconsidered.[31]

Wavell was scathing, telling Freyberg he considered the plan was possibly a cover for attack on Cyprus, Syria or Iraq, and that Freyberg's estimate of the scale of air attack was 'excessive'.[32] It is possible that Wavell was not aware that the material on which the original appreciation was based had actually come via ULTRA. He assured Freyberg that '. . . the Commander in Chief, Mediterranean, is prepared to support you if Crete is attacked'.[33] However, despite a stunning victory on 28–29 March against the Italian navy off Cape Matapan, Cunningham was not in a good position. His sole carrier was short on fighters, there were 'no reserves of naval aircraft or flying personnel', and he could not provide local air superiority in Cretan waters. He believed the island could be held against 'airborne assault only' and because of enemy air superiority could 'not commit our forces to the northward of Crete during daylight unless enemy forces were known to be at sea'.[34] This almost certainly contributed to Freyberg's evaluation that there was 'no evidence of naval forces capable of *guaranteeing* us against seaborne invasion'.[35]

Freyberg realised that the air component of the assault was likely to be the most critical, and responded with plans for a dynamic defence, maximising the effectiveness of his limited forces through speed of response and movement. CREFORCE Operation Instruction 10 of 3 May warned of air attack against the aerodromes 'and vicinity', supported by seaborne attack 'close to aerodromes and/or to Suda Bay'.[36] There was no doubt in Freyberg's mind that the German plan relied on early capture of the aerodromes. As he later wrote, the 'two aerodromes Maleme and Heraklion, and the Retimo landing

ground, dictated the siting of the military garrisons'.[37] Deployments were organised to suit this priority, and although potential sea landing spaces were to be watched, they were to be held by troops only 'if resources permit'.[38] The whole theme was rapid and 'spirited defence'.[39]

Surprise was an important element of the scheme, and the next day Freyberg exhorted his men to camouflage their positions against 'intensive aerial recce'.[40] This was passed through the chain of command and emerged in the deployments, for instance a training directive from the New Zealand Divisional headquarters issued to the forces defending Maleme, which ordered exercises 'in areas where units are likely to be employed, against air and airborne attack . . .

HMS *Formidable*, the Mediterranean Fleet's only aircraft carrier, was prevented from entering the battle directly by a critical shortage of Fulmar naval fighter aircraft. It is questionable whether the dozen or so Fulmars she could carry would have made much impact because, although effective against bombers, the Fulmar had only modest performance compared to land-based fighters.

Trent Corbett Collection

Concealment from the air will be practised at all times.'[41]

As a result of these plans, Freyberg was able to tell Churchill on 5 May that he was 'not in the least anxious about airborne attack'. He had made his dispositions and felt he could 'cope adequately with the troops now at my disposal'. But he remained concerned about a simultaneous combined assault. 'If that comes before I get the guns and transport here the situation will be difficult.'[42] The real purpose of this message was to signal that he needed high-level intercession to get what he needed to defend the island against both sea and air attack.[43] All would be well, Freyberg explained, 'when we get our equipment and the transport and . . . a few extra fighter aircraft', but meantime 'there will be a period here during which we shall be vulnerable'.[44]

Churchill took the signal seriously. A 'Tiger' convoy was taking much-needed tanks to Alexandria, and Churchill tried to divert part of it to Suda Bay. He was dissuaded by his 'expert colleagues' who thought it would be too risky given the German air bombardment. As a compromise on 9 May, Churchill suggested Wavell should send a dozen tanks on the *Clan Lamont* 'as soon as she has discharged her cargo at Alexandria'. Wavell had already made similar arrangements two days earlier.[46] On the 10th, Churchill decided Freyberg should be given a free hand to make use of ULTRA material.[47]

Freyberg received further information during the first two weeks of May, some of it speculative, which provided further detail of the German plans.[48] He continued to refine his defences, particularly in the critical Maleme–Canea sector, where on 11 May he established a new group that included 4 NZ Infantry Brigade — less 20 NZ Battalion — and a Composite Battalion, among other units. This was intended as a 'mobile reserve' specifically to back up the Maleme airfield defence and, if possible, watch the coast.[49] There was no doubt about the air priority. A divisional instruction of 13 May required 20 Battalion, Oakes Force and 6 Greek Battalion, plus some minor supporting units, to '. . . (a) . . . hold a

Allied Positions near Canea
20 May 1941

Akrotiri Peninsula

Hill 107

Engineer detachment

Theodhori

To Kastelli

Maleme airfield

Northumberland Hussars

22 Bn
Pirgos
Maleme
Maleme

Platanias

Canea

1 Welch

Bridge

28 (Maori) Bn
Composite Battalion
4 BDE

1 Rangers

Tavronitis River

23 Bn
5 BDE

Stalos

2NZ Div HQ

21 Bn

Platianas River
Galatas

Suda Bay

Xamoudokhori

Prison
19 AUSTRALIAN BDE

Suda

6 Greek Regiment

"42nd Street"

Episkon

2 Greek Regiment

8 Greek Regiment

To Sphakia

Built up areas

Main roads

Approximate German drop areas
(for specifics see detail maps)

defensive posn. facing west . . .' — in other words facing any troops that might come down west of Maleme — and, secondarily, '. . . (b) to defend the coast against invasion between north and south grid line 10 and excl. cape 033582'.[50]

Wavell sent Brigadier Eric Dorman-Smith to see Freyberg the next day, possibly to advise that further 'reliable information' was coming, but mainly to discuss the defences and canvass Freyberg's opinions.[51] After the 12 May meeting Freyberg again advised Wavell that he 'felt confident of defeating an air attack', but if the attack included a simultaneous 'beach landing with tanks', then 'we shall not be in a strong position'.[52]

This essentially repeated what he had told Churchill the week before; by making the comment Freyberg was again underlining, for the record, that he had been given insufficient equipment to meet a combined attack. However, it was only a discussion point — he remained clear in his understanding that the German plan hung on successful early seizure of the airfields by paratroop assault. The full 'Appreciation — German Plan for attack on Crete' which he issued the same day via his general staff was explicit:

The first objective will most certainly be the three aerodromes Heraklion, Retimo and Maleme . . . if the aerodromes hold out, as they will, the whole [German] plan will fail

. . . Although this appreciation has not mentioned sea landings on beaches, the possibility of these attacks must not be overlooked; but they will be of secondary importance to those from the air.[53]

The fresh ULTRA information which Freyberg received on 13 May was derived directly from 'operation orders issued', and it has been suggested that this may have been available to the British as much as a week before Freyberg saw it.[54] However, it was entirely in line with the signals of 29 April, adding detail and numbers to the already known thrust of the German plan.[55] Freyberg now learned that the German 7 Air Division would 'make a parachute landing and seize Maleme, Candia [Heraklion] and Retimo . . . dive bombers and fighters . . . will move by air to Maleme and Candia . . . Air landing of 11th Air Corps, including Corps Headquarters . . . probably including the 22nd division.' A 'seaborne contingent' would also land on the first day, bringing 'anti-aircraft batteries as well as . . . more troops and supplies . . .' apparently including 'motor cyclists, armoured units' and 'anti-tank units'.[56] The signal confirmed Freyberg's understanding of what was coming, and he urged his men to accept and use the information he had already issued. 'The contents of the [12 May] Appreciation must be digested,' he wrote to Brigadier Chappel on 14 May, 'and then it must be burnt.'[57] He reinforced the airfields with the

Matilda I tanks as they arrived, reporting to Wavell on the 16th that: 'Two infantry tanks are at each aerodrome.'[58]

Responsibility for specific field deployments rested on Freyberg's commanders. The Maleme–Canea sector itself was defended by the New Zealanders. Maleme — which was to Elliott a 'rotten little aerodrome'[59] — went to 5 Brigade under Brigadier James Hargest, a veteran of the First World War and MP for Southland when war broke out. He had volunteered his services in 1940. Freyberg was apparently reluctant to take him on, but Hargest appealed to Fraser for political intercession.[60] His brigade included 22 Battalion under First World War VC-winner Lieutenant Colonel L.W. Andrew, deployed on Maleme airfield, backed to the east by 21 and 23 Battalions and an Engineer Detachment.[61] A mobile reserve further east at Platanias was provided by 28 (Maori) Battalion.

5 Brigade was ordered to 'maintain a defensive line running east and west from Platanias to Tavronitis River with special regard to the defence of Maleme aerodrome'.[62] Freyberg clearly had an excellent appreciation of the difficulties, but there is evidence that his orders were not properly implemented by the field commanders at Maleme, though Hargest for one was confident. As early as 2 May, when first advised that Maleme was a target, Hargest believed he had the zone 'well defended' and 'will put up a great fight'.[63] He certainly had confidence in his own abilities, telling his wife on 10 May that 'in a crisis my judgement is sound and my instincts right'.[64] However, Freyberg's biographers Laurie Barber and John Tonkin-Covell have convincingly argued that, at a key meeting of 5 Brigade commanders next day in the Maleme courthouse, Hargest passed on Freyberg's instruction for prompt counter-attack, without apparently appreciating the terrain facing his battalion and company commanders.[65]

By 13 May, Hargest was doing his best 'to put some go into the work of defence'. He and Puttick inspected the western defences of Maleme that day. Although Hargest confided to his diary that Puttick 'seemed pleased',[66] there was actually a potential problem. Forces were deployed above the Tavronitis River, but not on the bed itself. Puttick and Freyberg discussed moving 1 Greek Regiment from Kastelli to the riverbed to defend it directly, but for various reasons the regiment was not moved. In the event the riverbed turned out to be a crucial German landing zone, and the decision not to move the Greeks drew attention. In 1952, Freyberg explained that Puttick had inspected the ground and concluded it would take too long for the regiment to dig in before the invasion, particularly as the Greeks lacked adequate tools.[67] It was also possible, as Barber and Tonkin-Covell noted, that the differing

New Zealand ingenuity at work. This picture is from the Greek campaign and shows General Freyberg's well-hidden office truck near Thermopylae. In Crete the same kind of camouflage skill frustrated German efforts to find New Zealand positions from the air. This particular photograph was later used in British training pamphlets.

Sir John White Collection

command structures meant permission to move the regiment took some time to obtain, making it impossible to redeploy them before the expected date of invasion.[68] Freyberg's son and biographer Paul Freyberg raised a third argument in 1991, that Freyberg wanted to strengthen the defences west of Maleme but was forbidden by Wavell because information pointing to a primary air attack was sourced solely from the ULTRA 'scale of attack' message. Deployment based on this sole source was forbidden for fear of compromising it.[69]

All these issues likely played a part, but in fact prior to the battle the Tavronitis valley was one of several areas, like Prison Valley, which happened to be outside the area of the concealed positions. Like other areas outside the immediate perimeter, Freyberg envisaged the Tavronitis could be protected by a mobile and 'spirited' defence. He was confident that his commanders properly appreciated this requirement.

The Germans observed the defensive preparations but learned little of value, complaining that:

All works were camouflaged with great skill. They were not discovered even on large scale air maps, or by eye during low flying recce. Several AA points, recognised from interpretation of air photos, proved to be dummy positions with wooden guns. The occupied AA positions were elsewhere and carefully camouflaged.[70]

Equipment shortages

Freyberg's main problem — as emerged time and again in his messages to his superiors — was his chronic shortage of equipment, which seriously undermined the effectiveness of his forces.[71] He tackled the supply issue with his usual thoroughness, even taking the fight right up to Churchill. Fraser was aware of the problem by 2 May, advising Churchill that New Zealand troops should 'either be supplied with sufficient means to defend the island, or that the decision to hold Crete at all costs should be reviewed'.[72] Nash meanwhile told Freyberg he was making every effort to locate and send 'additional motor equipment' from New Zealand.[73] On 3 May, Churchill hinted to Fraser that the Germans were only 'feinting at Crete' but was otherwise scathing; they had to 'consider all contingencies in the employment of our scant and overpressed air force'.[74] This was not what Fraser wanted to hear, and he left New Zealand next day for the Middle East to see what he could do himself.

Aircraft certainly were short; the British were, as Wavell put it, 'going through a lean period as regards fighter aircraft'.[75] Rommel was knocking on the doors of Egypt, and the British could not strip their African front to save Crete. There was a crisis in Iraq. Wavell confided to Freyberg that this was 'giving me a lot of trouble and I don't like it'.[76] The obsolete Gladiators and handful of

Hurricanes finally deployed to Crete put up a 'heroic performance' which was 'beyond praise', shooting down 32 aircraft — including nine 'unconfirmed' — and damaging 41 others.[77] However, they were outclassed and outnumbered, and Freyberg sent the seven surviving aircraft back to Cairo on 19 May 'to avoid useless loss of lives of the pilots who had fought gallantly against tremendous odds'.[78] This was not known to the Germans, who credited themselves with having 'decisively impeded the enemy's employment of air forces'.[79]

Once the aircraft had gone there was an opportunity to improve the island's defences by making the airfields unusable. This was not done, however, and Freyberg revealed the reasoning in a letter to Middle East Force headquarters in September that year:

The sole reason for not . . . [obstructing the airfields] . . . was that at the conference on the co-operation of the Army, Navy and Air Force held at Canea on 12th May 1941, it was decided that the role of the RAF was to reduce the scale of enemy attack, and to make this practicable the Air Officer Commanding made it clear that none of the three aerodromes should be permanently obstructed. Although the few remaining fighters were ordered to Egypt just before the battle, the intention was that fighters should return as soon as possible and make use of the aerodromes. In point of fact Heraklion was so used. I agree with the conclusion of the Committee that mining of the aerodromes, though it might have delayed the enemy, would not have effected [sic] the ultimate result.[80]

Freyberg also wanted food not only for his troops but also the islanders, prisoners and Greek refugees — over 400,000 souls in all. This did not prove possible, but he managed to procure mortars and machine guns, sixteen Vickers light tanks, six obsolete Matilda I infantry tanks, and rifles. Some of the latter were newly rebuilt, which caused problems as they had not been 'shot in'. Most of the material had to come in through the main harbour of Suda Bay, where enemy air superiority made unloading a hazardous business. Commanding officer Lieutenant Colonel G.J. McNaught found morale around the docks was 'rather low' as a result of frequent air raids. Port facilities were chaotic, there were 'no mobile or other cranes, narrow jetty with a goods shed partly damaged, jetty half covered with naval and RAF material'.[81] The harbour was quickly littered with wrecked freighters. J.K. Elliott, at CREFORCE headquarters, wrote in his diary that the 'methodical Hun' always 'used the same technique' and reliably turned up at 5 p.m.:

Before the Blitz, Canea Harbour was a mass of fishing boats, caiques and coasters.

Sir John White Collection

Ships on fire in Suda Bay after a dive-bombing attack. HMS York is on the left.
Sir John White Collection

The system of air raid warning was good — listening devices detected aircraft about ten minutes out to sea. The ringing of the church bells was the actual alarm and there were as many churches in Crete as there are pubs in Westport . . . The dive bombers came down from the west out of the sun. There were usually about thirty of them, and they screamed down in succession upon the ships and jetty and village. The Suda AA defences were as good as AA defences can be, and they put up a barrage which looked unbearable. The dive bombers went clean through the high barrage and down into the darker Bofors bursting stuff. These grand little guns pumped up their white hot looking tracer shells and it was they who got what Huns were shot down. In the later stages the Bofors gunners were magnificent.[82]

A particularly heavy raid on the morning of 14 May marked the beginning of an intense softening up prior to the parachute landings. That day the Luftwaffe targeted the cruiser HMS *York* — which, although seriously damaged in Suda harbour by an earlier Italian torpedo attack, still had an operational anti-aircraft battery. Amid the storm of steel the Dutch freighter *Nieuw Zeeland* arrived to unload men and equipment, including official war artist Peter McIntyre and the Kiwi Concert Party.

Communications were another issue. Most of the wireless equipment had been abandoned in Greece. Brigade and battalion signals sections laid telephone cables during the first weeks of May. Despite 'great difficulty' borrowing transport, they obtained 'cable, drum barrow, and few other supplies'. Important lines were duplicated, including one to the isolated 5 Brigade position at Maleme. The main line was strung along civilian telephone poles, but the duplicate had to be laid partly on the ground. It was not possible 'without great expenditure of time and material to provide more independent circuits'. Later, German paratroopers systematically cut the lines — coiling the lengths and throwing them into trees — while other links were broken by bomb and mortar fire.[83]

Freyberg was very busy during the lead-up to the invasion inspecting his forces and on 16 May reported to Wavell reported that he had:

. . . completed plans for defence of Crete and have just returned from final tour of defences. I feel greatly encouraged by my visits. Everywhere all ranks are fit and moral [sic] *is now high . . . I do not wish to seem over-confident but I feel that at least we will give an excellent account of ourselves. With help of Royal Navy I trust Crete will be held.*[84]

Privately he nevertheless retained 'grave doubts of our ability to hold Crete', writing a few weeks later that 'my statements that we would repel any enemy attack, were made with the intention of raising the morale of the troops'.[85]

The air attacks built up to a crescendo, particularly over Maleme. Freyberg was very concerned about the men. 'The men must stick this bombardment which is more frightening than effective.' He had no intention of keeping them in the dark about it. 'The Appreciation must get down to the men,' he told Brigadier Chappel on 14 May; 'they are to be warned.'[86] Most of the Kiwis consequently knew what was coming, though rumour distorted the numbers. 'Expect 10,000 by sea — 25,000 by air — landing at 5 points,' James Pickett wrote two days later. 'That means us. Big raid again. Looks like we're for it.'[87] His unit was posted to reserve for two days on 18 May. 'What a relief,' he wrote, 'now for some sleep ... I shall start a long letter home. Better reply to my mail first.'[88]

The Luftwaffe had uninterrupted control of the skies during the Crete campaign, bombing and strafing at will. This Stuka had just attacked Suda and, as it left heading south, overflew CREFORCE head-quarters.

Sir John White Collection

AIRBORNE ASSAULT
20 MAY 1941

German soldiers approach their transports, ready for the assault on Crete. This picture is one of several found on a soldier's camera captured by New Zealanders during the battle. The fact that troops are loading in daylight makes it probable that this photo was taken on 21–22 May.

Jim Seymour Collection

. . . men who I have known . . . have become heroes — others have shown remarkable qualities unsuspected hitherto . . . Our positions were slashed and torn to pieces but they held . . . The men went into action like heroes . . . NOTHING could be finer than the Maoris . . . We partly succeeded but the odds were too great. I believe that no troops in the world could have done better or as well.

— Brigadier James Hargest to his wife, 24 May 1941[1]

In the pre-dawn hours of 20 May, the airfields around Athens and on Milos Island reverberated to the shattering roar of aircraft engines. Darkness meant nothing to the men; the troops of XII and VII Fleigerkorps made their way to their aircraft illuminated only by the glow of the exhausts. At Tangara, Student spoke briefly with his glider pilots, a last-minute personal touch that lifted the spirits of men facing the unknown. One by one the bombers and transports taxied to the runways. As the first hint of dawn flushed the sky they began to take off. In the darkness and dust some had to abort and try later. But by daybreak all were on their way to Crete.

The German plan divided Crete into three sectors — Komet, Mars and Orion. The first assault group, under Major General Werner Meindl, was directed against Maleme and spearheaded by three glider detachments of about 500 men each. They were tasked with capturing the Tavronitis bridge, knocking out the AA guns near the rivermouth, and taking the tactically important high ground near the airfield — Kavzakia Hill, Point 107 on the tactical maps. Parachutists were to move quickly to support the glider units.

AIRBORNE ASSAULT

Above: **German paratroopers pose proudly in front of their aircraft.**

Jim Seymour Collection

Left: **German infantry boarding a Junkers Ju 52/3m. Each carries a 7.62 mm Mauser Kar 98K, the standard German infantry rifle of both world wars. Although accurate and robust, it had a difficult bolt-action, and by 1941 was being replaced by various automatic weapons such as the MP-38/40. These were extensively used in Crete.**

Jim Seymour Collection

Above: **Paratroop training was made as tough and realistic as possible, but still did not match the reality of dropping into enemy-held territory. Paratroops seldom had the luxury of being able to neatly deflate their parachutes before scurrying for cover — men behaving as seen here were picked off at once on Crete.**

Trent Corbett Collection

SPECIFICATIONS
Junkers Ju 52/3m g3e

Power plant: three BMW 132-A-3 radial air-cooled engines developing TO power of 725 hp.

Armament: 1 x 7.9 mm MG15 machine gun with 1050 rounds, 1 x 7.9 mm MG15 with 750 rounds in ventral turret, up to ten 110 pound SC50 or two 551 pound SC250 bombs.

Performance: maximum speed: 165 mph at sea level; maximum continuous cruise: 153 mph at 3000 feet; range on maximum fuel: 620 miles; service ceiling 19,360 feet.

Cargo: up to eighteen fully equipped troops, or cargo.

Weights: empty: 12,610 pounds; normal load 20,944 pounds; maximum overload 23,146 pounds.

Span: 95 feet 11½ inches

Length: 62 feet

Height: 18 feet 2½ inches

Jim Seymour Collection

A Junkers Ju 52/3m transport readying for the attack on Crete. Known affectionately as 'TxJu' (Aunty Ju) to the Germans, the Junkers Ju 52 was designed by Ernst Zindel as a single-engine transport and first flew in 1930. A three-engine variant, the Ju 52/3m flew in 1931 and was so successful that production switched entirely to this model. After a combat debut as a bomber in the Spanish Civil War of 1936 the Ju 52/3m came into its own as a general-purpose transport. In late 1937 the XII *Fleigerdivision* (*Fallschirmjager*) (paratroops) formed on the type. In April the following year the unit was re-designated *Kampfgruppe zur besonderen Verwendung* 1 (Battle Wing for Special Duties 1), usually abbreviated to K.Gr.z.b.V.1.

In January 1941, three new *Transportgruppen* (Transport Wings), K.Gr.z.b.V. 40, 50 and 60 were formed with the Ju 52/3m to support military operations in the Greek theatre, joining other units in the field. The assault on

Crete was conducted by units of K.Gr.z.b.V. 40, 105 and 106, forming KG.z.b.V.1, and by K.Gr.z.b.V. 60, 101 and 102, 1/KG.z.b.V.1 and I/LLG 1. These latter units formed KG.z.b.V.2. Reserves included I *Gruppe* (wing) and part of II *Gruppe*, including G.G.z.b.V. 172, backed by four *Staffeln* (Squadrons) of the towplane variant and LLG.1. *Stab* (staff).

Some 271 Junkers were lost over Crete, nearly half the total assault force. In early June most of the Junkers forces were withdrawn from the Mediterranean theatre in preparation for the assault on the Soviet Union three weeks later. Attrition of the type that year exceeded production. Even then the type was obsolescent, and more modern replacements such as the Ju 252 and Ju 352 were developed, but demand for transport aircraft remained so high that the Ju 52/3m remained in production until mid-1944. It was still in service with the Spanish air force as late as the 1960s.

Komet sector — Maleme, Tavronitis and Point 107

The air strength against us has been overwhelming. The whole fighting area has been so strongly blitzed with m.g. fire & bombs from the air that our tps have not had a fair chance . . .
— Lieutenant Colonel William Gentry to his wife,
29 May 1941[2]

The New Zealanders saw the attack as a dark line of aircraft sweeping low over the sea. Few were privy to Freyberg's Ultra intelligence — in his headquarters on the slopes above Canea, where he could see the whole battlefield from Maleme to Canea, he murmured 'right on time'. Most of the 180 fighters, 150 Stukas and 180 level bombers went towards Maleme, where the Bf 109's and twin-engined Bf 110's raked the ground with machine-gun and cannon fire. Stukas and Dornier level bombers followed. At Platanias, Hargest was strafed as he tried to reach his headquarters trench. He looked across to Maleme to see that the aerodrome was a 'mass of flame & smoke & dust'.[3]

The raid ended around 7.30 and the men stood down for breakfast, but about twenty minutes later the airfield came under even more intense assault. Andrew was slightly wounded by a splinter. Just as the chaos reached its peak the first gliders swept in, coming under fire from the New Zealanders. Nine landed in the dry riverbed south of the Tavronitis bridge, disgorging elements of the

Headquarters Battalion under Major Braun. Others, carrying 3 Company under Lieutenant Plessen, landed north of the bridge. The riverbed was out of the direct line of fire of the 22 Battalion forces dug in above, and as a result the two German groups were able to seize the bridge.

Air defences around Maleme included ten Bofors and two 3-inch anti-aircraft guns, but the heavier weapons could not fire effectively below 300 feet, and many aircraft came in lower. The parachutists arrived hard on the heels of the gliders. J.N. Kinder had a good view from Galatas ridge as 'plane after plane came in in a seemingly endless line at a height of no more than 100 feet and sailed majestically over the aerodrome and dropped their loads'.[4] From Creforce headquarters, J.K. Elliott:

A grounded DFS 230 assault glider on Crete, with a dead soldier lying under the wing. The DFS 230A-1/2 variant was replaced in production during late 1940 by the stronger DFS 230B-1/2, which was also fitted with a braking parachute. Typical cargo was 2734 pounds, usually ten fully equipped men and 600 pounds of freight.

DA1156 Kippenberger Military Archive & Research Library, Army Museum, Waiouru

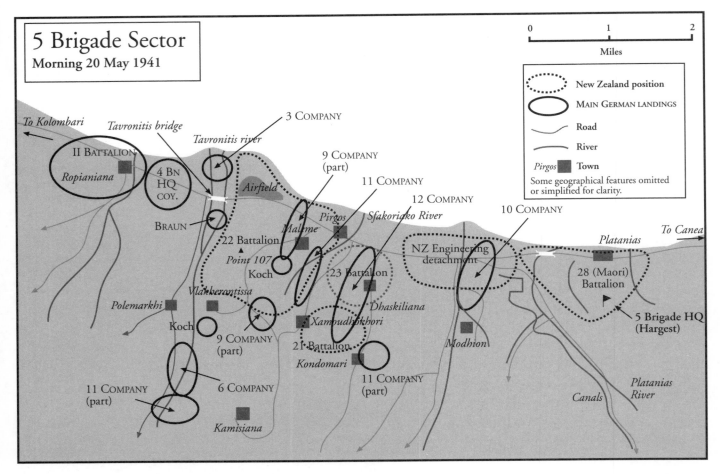

5 Brigade Sector
Morning 20 May 1941

. . . saw the black dots fall from each plane and almost at once the parachute would open and along the track of the plane would be . . . a line of falling white parachutes — about sixteen per plane . . . Some of the parachutes were coloured — I saw a few bright red ones, and the idea was that the officers' parachutes should be readily distinguishable as a rallying point. Other coloured parachutes marked weapons such as mortars, stores and

ammunition. The organisation was perfect — it was one of those things that I thought just could not happen and here I was looking at it.[5]

To Lieutenant Colonel W.G. Gentry, Senior Operations Officer of the New Zealand Division, the landings 'seemed more like something one sees in the films'. He did not think much of the technique, writing that 'in most cases' the parachutists were 'killed within a few minutes. In some places they actually landed right in the areas occupied by troops & most of those were accounted for before they reached the ground.' But their preparations drew admiration:

They were beautifully equipped. A great deal of forethought & energy has gone into the air force division. We have nothing like it. They also landed in glider & finally in troop carrying aircraft. The noise was terrific.[6]

Many defenders opened fire with rifles and Bren guns, riddling the transports and doing terrible execution. Soldier after soldier died in the air, a few even before jumping, but some defenders felt that firing on helpless Germans was unsporting and let the paratroopers land safely. Some landings were chaotic. Six hundred men of the German 3 Battalion missed their area northeast of Maleme because of the wind. A few were blown out to sea and drowned, while others came down around the New Zealand Engineers, 23 Battalion, and 22 Battalion on the airfield itself. The Germans suffered 400 casualties within the first three-quarters of an hour. Most could not reach their equipment packs.

The fact that so many parachutists landed in defended areas was a testament to Freyberg's deployments, and to the camouflage skills of the New Zealanders. The Germans 'were surprised that parachutists . . . could be hit by riflemen on

the ground'.[7] Interviewing Oberfeldweber (Sergeant Major) F. Teichmann of the Meindl Sturm (Assault) Regiment at the end of 1945, W.G. McClymont was told:

Each parachutist had a pistol, grenades, a machine pistol or a rifle and ammunition, each had six days' food. They wore a parachutist's jacket over ordinary uniform. Motor cycles were dropped and small guns 10 cm . . . Personally, like all parachutists who landed on Crete . . . [Teichmann] *did not think they were properly equipped. Their clothing was too heavy and it was incredibly hot running through the vineyards. They should have had suitable gear for that type of fighting. And they had too many weapons, everything was too heavy . . . Water was very difficult to obtain and they were often very thirsty.*[8]

German paratroops come in over Crete. The extreme low altitude of the 'drop' is evident from this view, which also reveals the degree to which descending troops were scattered as they came down. Most were easily picked off by well-positioned defenders.

1992.1697 Kippenberger Military Archive & Research Library, Army Museum, Waiouru

ABOVE: **The real thing — German paratroops dropping into enemy-held territory. The neat formations quickly disintegrated under fire from the New Zealanders.**

Trent Corbett Collection

ABOVE: **For the Germans the first day of battle was one of slaughter. The parachutists descended with only minimal gear; most of what they needed was dropped separately. Ordinarily they would have had no real problem reaching these containers, but on Crete many were ambushed and killed before they got to them.**

Trent Corbett Collection

The landing on the slopes of Point 107 failed; gliders carrying 1 Battalion HQ company and elements of 4 Company to the target were separated and pinned down by the New Zealanders. The German official diarist later noted admiringly that the 'enemy, New Zealand sharp shooters, held their strongly organised and well camouflaged defensive localities with the utmost determination'.[9] Meindl landed at around 8.30 a.m. and realised his plan had gone awry. By this time other elements of 2 Battalion had landed west of the Tavronitis. The Fourth Battalion came down even further west, fought its way through civilian resistance, and moved to join its fellows. The Second Battalion landed over Ropianiana, west of the Tavronitis valley.

The field telephone lines were an early German target, forcing Andrew to rely on runners. West of the airfield the defences were thin. Lieutenant R.B. Sinclair, commanding 15 Platoon, had only 22 men to cover a 1500-yard front; and 22 Platoon was not much better off. By about 10 a.m. the Germans had made steady inroads. Andrew refused a request to deploy his tanks — two Mk I Matildas — and the two 4-inch guns near Canea could not be brought to bear, but he was able to get artillery fire down on the German positions. By 2.55 p.m. the Germans had penetrated the perimeter of Andrew's headquarters unit, and at 3.50 p.m. he made an urgent call to Hargest for reinforcements.

Some German paratroops of 3 Battalion came down too far north of their intended position and were blown out to sea, where they drowned.

1990.1749 Kippenberger Military Archive & Research Library, Army Museum, Waiouru

Canea and Suda Bay

The Jerry planes had been flying around as thick as flies for an hour and a half bombing and machine gunning anywhere and everywhere, covering the island in a pall of dust and smoke, then we saw the first of the huge Junkers flying slowly through the murky atmosphere. We knew what to expect and weren't so very much surprised when we saw them drop out — the 'umbrella men' as one Greek woman described them. Out they dropped, one by one, their parachutes opening as soon as they had left the plane, 12 to 18 men to a plane.

— J.E.J. WESTBROOK, 17 JUNE 1941[10]

Student intended to seize Canea and Suda docks, but assault commander General Suessman became the first casualty when the glider he and his headquarters unit were travelling in suffered structural failure and crashed on Aegina.[11] Captain Altmann's assault regiment, meant to come down on the Akrotiri Peninsula and knock out the anti-aircraft batteries, was engaged by the batteries as it approached. Some of the gliders crashed. The rest landed, and the disembarking men were attacked by the Northumberland Hussars. Most were killed

but a few escaped and what Elliott called 'a sort of guerrilla warfare' followed:

The Huns used to hide up in the rocks and snipe Force HQ — they did not do much damage but we could not spare the troops to clean them out. They used to sneak down at night and have pot shots and get water. There were not enough of them to be a serious threat . . . They used to fire Verey lights at night to show their pals out at Maleme where they were. [12]

The attack by Lieutenant Gentz on 234 HAA Battery south of Canea was more successful. He landed with five out of nine gliders and took the guns, but was unable to attack a radio post south of the battery.

The ridge near Galatas was held by the New Zealand 19 Battalion and part of a composite battalion. Most of 18 Battalion, under Lieutenant Colonel J.R. Gray, was deployed in olive groves on each side of the

Top: One of the best-known pictures from the battle of Crete — Freyberg and his ADC Jack Griffiths outside the protective wall around his headquarters, where they had gone to get a better view of the bombing.
Sir John White Collection

Middle: This is the General's view of the battlefield area, from Galatas to Maleme with Canea in the foreground, under full-scale bombardment from the air.
Sir John White Collection

Bottom: This is the same view after the attack was over.
Sir John White Collection

coast road not far from Canea. Gray watched one group come down nearby and led his headquarters company against them — mobilising everybody including the cook. Even the officers had rifles. Gray wounded one paratrooper who was hiding behind a tree, approached the 'very frightened' man, and 'told him to lie still and he would be looked after'.[13] Once he had secured the area, Gray returned to his headquarters and was in the middle of shaving when Inglis ordered him to reinforce 7 General Field Hospital, down the road to the west and under heavy German attack.

This hospital and the nearby 6 Field Ambulance was one of the primary German objectives. Despite the large red crosses it had been mistaken for a tented military camp. The attack began as 'an extraordinarily fierce aerial bombardment and machine gunning'.[14] Westbrook saw one glider fly 'low over us' which, 'to all appearances, looked perfectly harmless', and concluded that the gliders were probably only there to 'attract AA fire'. He found it 'an uncanny experience to have that glider passing over our heads. It was an immense thing and it made no noise but a swish swishing sound.'[15]

10 Company under Lieutenant Pagels was dropped near the hospital by Junkers. They suffered casualties on the way down, but quickly organised an attack that captured about 100 medical personnel and 40 patients. Westbrook saw 'some of the patients clearing down to the beach while a figure in white, a nurse, disappeared over a hill'.[16] He was horrified to discover that the Germans had taken:

. . . as many 'walking' wounded as they could and were using them as shields as they advanced towards our lines, but by clever shooting of our boys and the heroic co-operation and guidance of a major who was one of the walking wounded and who ducked the fire that came from our lines, the Jerries' dirty trick failed . . .[17]

The Germans probably realised they had found a hospital, but officially never admitted their error, persistently referring to the hospital as a 'tented camp' and boasting of 500 prisoners. By the same token, it appears the early impression among the Kiwis that the Germans had used patients as human shields was also mistaken; the 'dirty trick' was also disputed by a later New Zealand investigation.[18] The patients were rescued by the New Zealanders. 'Exposed during the day to fierce enemy counter-attacks,' the German war diary noted, 'the company commander decided to abandon the tented camp and to break through to the Regiment in the direction of Galatas.' They ran into an ambush and Pagels 'was killed with the majority of his company'.[19] Elliott had a 'grandstand view' of the action from CREFORCE headquarters and thought the 'whole question of the Geneva Convention and protection of medical units is a vexed

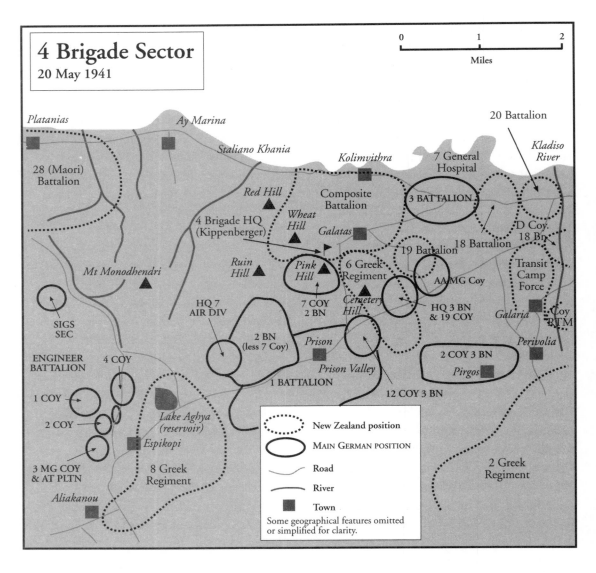

4 Brigade Sector
20 May 1941

0   1   2
Miles

Platanias
Ay Marina
Staliano Khania
Kolimvithra
20 Battalion
Kladiso River
28 (Maori) Battalion
7 General Hospital
Red Hill
Composite Battalion
3 BATTALION
4 Brigade HQ (Kippenberger)
Wheat Hill
Galatas
D Coy. 18 Bn
18 Battalion
Mt Monodhendri
Ruin Hill
Pink Hill
6 Greek Regiment
19 Battalion
Transit Camp Force
SIGS SEC
HQ 7 AIR DIV
7 COY 2 BN
AA MG Coy
Cemetery Hill
HQ 3 BN & 19 COY
Galaria
Coy RTM
ENGINEER BATTALION
4 COY
2 BN (less 7 Coy)
Prison
Perivolia
1 COY
1 BATTALION
Prison Valley
2 COY 3 BN
Pirgos
2 COY
Lake Aghya (reservoir)
3 MG COY & AT PLTN
Espikopi
8 Greek Regiment
12 COY 3 BN
2 Greek Regiment
Aliakanou

⋯ New Zealand position
◯ MAIN GERMAN POSITION
~ Road
— River
■ Town
Some geographical features omitted or simplified for clarity.

one'. In Crete, he felt, it was 'specially muddled — the 7th GH was undoubtedly on a site which was of tactical importance and should not have been there. On the other hand where should it have been?'[20]

The affair had a curious postscript. Early reports reaching Britain confused prisoners with combatants, causing Churchill to tell the House that the Germans were 'wearing New Zealand battle-dress'.[21]

The township of Galatas, on the hills south of the hospital, was another target. 'This is hell,' James Pickett scribbled in his pocket diary from his position near the town, his words barely keeping up with his racing thoughts. 'Even as I write the planes . . . never seen so many in all my life . . .'[22] J.N. Kinder watched Captain von der Heydte's 1 Battalion come in over Prison Valley:

Each plane dropped about 18 to 22 parachutes and as each plane emptied out it turned and sailed slowly past over our position and so out to sea. The air was full of parachutes and they certainly made a great target, although . . . out of range of our rifles. However I grabbed the anti-tank rifle, and took pot shots at the planes with it, but didn't see very many crash to the ground.[23]

This landing also went wrong — the Germans discovered at the last moment that the 'nature of the ground' where Parachute Rifle Regiment 3 landed had 'not been correctly appreciated from the available maps and air photographs'. The men were actually dropping into a valley.[24] Von der Heydte's force lost much of their equipment, but took the prison and advanced east against minimal Greek resistance. By chance they found 3 Battalion 11 Company, which had missed its landing around Galatas, and the two groups pushed as far as Mournies before falling back to Perivolia.

The German 2 Battalion came down northeast of the prison. Defence here hinged on Pink Hill, at the boundary between the Composite Battalion and the 6th Greek Regiment. The Greeks withdrew, forcing Kippenberger to move his headquarters back to Ruin Hill, but the day was saved by Petrol Company, which put up a stout defence. Soon afterwards Captain M. Forrester rallied the Greeks, who surged back into battle. Below the town, elements of the German 3 Battalion engaged part of the New Zealand 19 Battalion just as the men began breakfast.

J.N. Kinder was part of a platoon sent into Galatas to investigate reports of snipers around midday:

In the village square all was chaos. The Greek force had been holding the opposite side of the village and, although the enemy was well out

Canea under the blitz — a view from inside the parapet at CREFORCE headquarters.

Official war artist Peter McIntyre's interpretation of the Germans landing near Galatas. The Kiwis were fortunate to have such a talented artist on site; his drawings and paintings are a rare record of the defence of Crete. Thanks to a disastrous misreading of reconnaissance photography, the Germans actually landed in a valley below the village.

DA1403 Kippenberger Military Archive & Research Library, Army Museum, Waiouru

*of range, had blazed away all their ammun-
ition at the parachutes. Also the Jerries had
captured their dump, and their rifles were
consequently useless. They begged us for
ammunition but ours would not fit their rifles,*

*and anyhow I doubt if we would have given
them any. Any of them might have been the
snipers we were looking for.* [25]

By mid-afternoon it had become clear that the Germans were concentrating around the prison, and Kippenberger wanted to counter-attack. He did not get an answer from Puttick and by 7 p.m. was in some despair, scribbling a note for Puttick in pencil on squared exercise paper:

*. . . wire to you has been down for two hours
and enemy are at present within short range of
exchange . . . Please advise posn. and
instruct. I don't think this line would hold
against serious attack tomorrow.* [26]

Retimo and Heraklion were the focus of the second wave during the afternoon. This had to wait for the transports to return to Greece, where they were refuelled by hand. Many had been damaged by anti-aircraft and light arms fire, and a number had been shot down during the first attacks. Take-off was delayed by dust, but by 2.15 p.m. aircraft were in the air and returning to Crete, and the second assault began at about 4.15. Two battalions of 2 Parachute Regiment were dropped to capture Retimo. They were meant to move on to attack Suda, but were pinned by two Australian and four Greek battalions. Heraklion, further east, was defended by the British 14 Infantry Brigade of four battalions, plus some Greek forces.

The Germans came in under planned strength — a result of transport shortages — and suffered terrible losses. More than 500 were killed and many wounded.

These were not the only difficulties the Germans faced. They relied on air-dropped supplies, and their system was quickly subverted by the New Zealanders, as Elliott noted:

All the parachute troops carried swastika flags about 5 feet by 2 feet made of red silk with a black swastika in a white circle on the red field. They laid these out to establish their position and our troops soon had lots of these and laid them out to good effect. The air was continuously occupied . . . by circling DO17s and Henschel army cooperation planes . . . [examining] the ground in meticulous detail. The laying of the swastika flags was followed by these, and soon after mortars and ammunition food and medical supplies was dropped to the grateful troops below. The 19th told me that they had everything from folding bicycles to rolls of bumpf and packets of inferior cigarettes dropped on them by the far planning Hun.[28]

Captured German documents provided information about the German system for bringing parachute reinforcements down on rendezvous points. As a result 28 (Maori) Battalion in particular was able to lure unsuspecting German paratroopers into well-planned ambushes.

Bombs falling over Heraklion during the first day of battle.
Sir John White Collection

Parachutists over Heraklion.
Sir John White Collection

J.N. Kinder was among the volunteers called to probe German lines near Galatas as the first day of battle drew to a close. His memoir captures the reality of the battle as experienced by individual soldiers.

One party under Lieut Wilds was to work through the village while six of us under Sgt McCarthy . . . were to work along the side of the hill and connect up with the others later. Our own right flank was the ASG who did not know of our move. About 5 p.m. we set out and came out to an open piece of ground. Ahead . . . was a patch of crop which we thought would afford excellent cover . . . We only made one mistake but it almost cost us all our lives. It was a very still evening and every move we made was advertised by the moving of the crop. Suddenly a rifle spoke and Mac McCarthy fell. Owen Lee was next and then Basil Fisher got raked along the side. We were caught like rats in a trap so did the only thing possible and lay still. He missed me, but I think he thought I was done as he stopped firing. It was now almost dusk and we could only wait until it was dark enough to move. Suddenly we realised that the ASG on our right were retreating so we had to get out or get captured. Our first move brought a volley from our own men . . . The 20th then came through at the charge and relieved the position so we despatched two men for assistance while Len Simpson and I went back to collect our wounded. Owen Lee was able to walk, but Mac was hit pretty badly . . . The party in the village had not contacted us so we decided to take the wounded back and leave the 20th in possession. That trip was a nightmare and it wasn't till just at midnight that we got to the Regimental Aid Post about a mile from the gully . . . Mac I found out later died on the way to hospital, and so died one of the bravest soldiers and best men that I have ever served under. [27]

Anti-aircraft fire took a heavy toll on the low-flying Germans; two aircraft come to a fiery demise over Heraklion.

Sir John White Collection

Counter-attacks at Maleme

*Telephone communication was unreliable and
usually the lines were down due to bomb blast.
Practically no wireless equipment existed and
little visual signalling gear. The only way to
find out what was happening was to go and
look for yourself and in daylight this was not a
healthy occupation.*

— J.K. Elliott[29]

It became clear as the sun sank on 20 May
that the Germans had lodgements in Prison
Valley and west of Maleme. Andrew's
headquarters on Maleme airfield came
under mortar fire at around 4 p.m.. An hour
later he asked Hargest for support, but was
told that 23 Battalion was heavily engaged.
Andrew then decided to deploy his two
elderly Matilda Mk I infantry tanks,
supported by 14 Platoon. Independently, at
about 5.15 p.m., Hargest signalled divisional
headquarters that he was sending in two
companies, one from 23 Battalion and one
from 28 (Maori) Battalion.

This news did not reach Andrew, and in
any case Hargest's decision came too late —
the tanks were on their way. Their objective
was the Tavronitis road bridge, but the two
vehicles had not gone very far before the
first crew found they had been given the
wrong ammunition for the gun, and had to
pull out. The second tank reached the
riverbed and drove along it for perhaps 200
yards, engaging the Germans with its 2-

pounder, before bellying into a shallow pit.
The turret jammed and the crew had to
abandon the vehicle. Meanwhile 14 Platoon
was decimated by German light arms fire
and withdrew. This left the western
perimeter of the field held only by elements
of the battalion headquarters unit. At
around 6 p.m. Andrew informed Hargest
that he intended to withdraw to a ridge
adjacent to the airfield held by B Company.
Hargest seemed despondent. 'If you must,'
he told Andrew, 'you must.'[30] A few minutes
later he told Andrew that two companies
were on their way,[31] but the Maori did not
leave Platanias for another hour, when
Captain Rangi Royal led B Company —
made up of Te Arawa — down the road with
the aim of reoccupying Point 107.

They had almost reached 23 Battalion
near Pirgos when they encountered the first
of several groups of paratroopers. The
Germans offered to surrender, but then
hurled a grenade. The Maori retaliated with
a bayonet charge that killed twenty-four of
the enemy.[32] Two further short encounters
followed as Te Arawa advanced, now armed
with German weaponry including several
MP-38 sub-machine guns.[33] They reached
23 Battalion and were led towards the
airfield, speaking in Maori to avoid being
confused with Germans. As they
approached the airfield, however, they
encountered increasing opposition. Royal

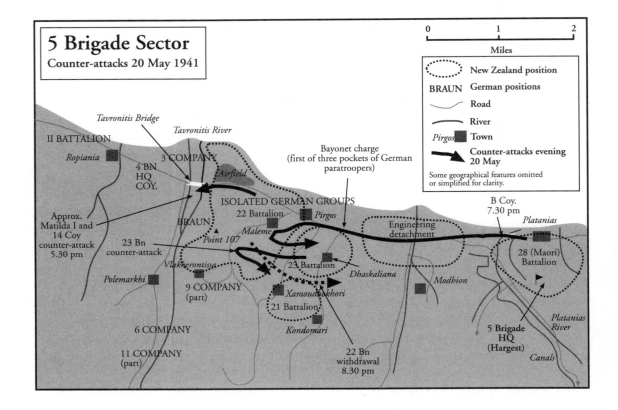

5 Brigade Sector
Counter-attacks 20 May 1941

0   1   2
Miles

········ New Zealand position
BRAUN German positions
 Road
 River
Pirgos ■ Town
➤ Counter-attacks evening
20 May
Some geographical features omitted
or simplified for clarity.

II BATTALION
Ropiania
Tavronitis Bridge
Tavronitis River
3 COMPANY
4 BN
HQ
COY.
Airfield
Bayonet charge
(first of three pockets of German
paratroopers)
B Coy.
7.30 pm
Platanias
ISOLATED GERMAN GROUPS
22 Battalion
Pirgos
Engineering
detachment
Approx.
Matilda I and
14 Coy
counter-attack
5.30 pm
BRAUN
Maleme
Point 107
23 Bn
counter-attack
23 Battalion
Dhaskaliana
Modhion
28 (Maori)
Battalion
Vlakherontissa
Polemarkhi
9 COMPANY
(part)
Xamoudakhori
21 Battalion
Kondomari
22 Bn
withdrawal
8.30 pm
5 Brigade
HQ
(Hargest)
*Platanias
River*
Canals
6 COMPANY
11 COMPANY
(part)

concluded that the airfield had fallen and pulled back, just missing 22 Battalion C Company.

Captain Carl Watson separately led 23 Battalion A Company towards Point 107, but they were fired on by a German machine gun and pulled back to Andrew's headquarters to regroup. Andrew held on until about 8.30 p.m., and with the batteries fading in the radio told Hargest he was pulling back to B Company's ridge. Here he found the Germans about to flank him. Apparently believing he had only two intact companies, he decided to pull back to 21 and 23 Battalion positions east of the airfield. This left the Germans essentially in possession of the airfield.

Hargest later bore the brunt of the blame for this outcome; he was killed in 1944, but this did not lessen service feeling about his performance at Maleme. After the war other hastened to his defence. 'Hargest may have made mistakes,' 23 Battalion official historian Angus Ross told Davin in 1949, 'but he evidently expected the main invasion to come from the sea.'[34] Ross had been transcribing Hargest's diaries and letters as part of the war history effort and was perhaps in the best position to understand Hargest's thinking.[35] Although his observation was intended to ameliorate criticism, it actually indicates that Hargest had misunderstood the main thrust of Freyberg's strategy, which relied on denying the airfields to the enemy first.

Hargest's apparent failure to co-ordinate 5 Brigade forces during the evening on 20 May was a contributing factor. Davin was of the opinion that had Hargest 'gone forward to 23 Battalion' he might have been able to 'launch a night counter-attack across the river,'[36] while Tony Simpson argued in his 1981 analysis that the key element was Hargest's failure to tell Andrew that he was sending elements of 23 and 28 Battalion into Maleme.[37] All these are valid points, and it seems clear that, quite apart from misunderstanding Freyberg's intentions, Hargest had not made the 'spirited defence' that Freyberg regarded as crucial. However, events must also be considered in the context of the breakdown of both tanks. This was not anticipated and essentially guaranteed the failure of the first counter-attack around 5 p.m. Communications and planning later in the evening were seriously hampered by the 'fog of war'. Andrew had been cut off from his companies for much of the day, and by 8.30 p.m. his contact with Hargest had gone, making effective co-ordination impossible. Andrew's perimeter had been beaten back, his tanks had failed, and the day was likely to bring further attacks from the air. The New Zealanders on the Maleme front did not realise the Germans had also been fought to a standstill. The Germans actually felt very vulnerable during the night of the 20th. Major Stenzler brought 5 and 7 Company to within about 1000 yards of Point 107 by evening, and knew there were other German units to the south, but they were nervy and unsettled. A single 'parting gift' in the form of a grenade as the New Zealanders left almost caused a stampede among Captain Walter Gericke's unit. When the Germans did take the hill, they were so short of ammunition they did not think they could hold it against a concerted counter-attack. A concerted effort by 23 Battalion could well have disrupted the German positions; but this is an observation of hindsight.

Overnight developments

We have had a hard day. Everything depends on the next few hours. The whole of my force has been in action. The importance of the battle is realised by us all.

— GENERAL FREYBERG TO PETER FRASER, 20 MAY 1941

By the end of the first day the battle hung in the balance. 'I believe that so far we hold the aerodromes at Maleme, Heraklion and Retimo and the two harbours,' Freyberg reported to Wavell. 'The margin by which we hold them is a bare one, and it would be wrong of me to paint an optimistic picture.'[38] His first priority was assessing likely German reinforcements. Force Intelligence Officer Robin Bell indicated that almost a whole parachute division had landed. As Elliott noted:

This meant they had no more available parachutists in the Balkans and that we could concentrate all our troops on those that had landed. Robin was right as we found out later. The English IO said he was not sure and asked to wire Middle East for the latest intelligence about the location of the two German parachutist divisions . . . The General said that if he was sure that all the parachutists had been landed he could gamble and get up most of the Retimo and Heraklion garrisons and counter-attack properly. He decided to wait further word from the Middle East . . .[39]

Geoffrey Cox then discovered an operational order in two sacks of captured German papers which had been earmarked for shipping to Cairo. He later wrote to Dan Davin that he '. . . started to look through the bundle of documents captured during the day, and came on a very faded undercopy of the operation order . . . This I translated for the General in his dugout . . .'[40]

This was a real coup. 'It showed that 1700 parachutists had landed around Maleme (one complete regiment) and that two further regiments had been landed by glider just to the westward,' Elliott wrote a few weeks after the battle. 'About the same number had been landed in the valley behind Canea.'[41] It confirmed the ULTRA intelligence Freyberg had received, particularly the fact that there were objectives for 'four groups, three of airborne parachutists and the fourth seaborne to reinforce the airborne attack on Maleme'.[42] In other words, Freyberg had been correctly informed about the attack, he had correctly deployed to meet it, and by these deployments the German plan had been defeated in all areas but Maleme. In 1950, Cox told Davin:

. . . had we known anything of the Order of Battle of the Airborne troops we could from this document have deduced that the enemy had virtually no parachutists in reserve, and

General Freyberg's driver, Sergeant Cropp, watches the smoke and dust during the last air raid of the day.
Sir John White Collection

have taken bigger risks the next day. As it was, the effect . . . was to convince [Freyberg] that the main attack had misfired, and that if Maleme were cleared all would be well . . . And we did learn from that Operation Order the cardinal fact that the Germans had grossly underestimated our strength on the island.[43]

However, the opportunity to counter-attack at Maleme that night was lost — something that was not known in CREFORCE.[44] Andrew reached 23 Battalion headquarters before 2 a.m. on 21 May. A runner was sent to inform Hargest and 21 Battalion commander Lieutenant Colonel Allen. The three Battalion commanders held a conference about an hour

later, deciding to hold their positions but not to counter-attack. This ran against Freyberg's orders to 'counter attack and destroy . . . immediately'.[45] They may have felt they were not in a position to make the 'spirited defence' Freyberg intended, although as Davin noted, only 22 Battalion had suffered significantly. Hargest apparently wanted to attack, but when he met Andrew he simply ordered his units into the defensive line with the others. His concern that German air superiority would be decisive after dawn may have been a factor; but it is also possible that air bombardment all day had sapped his strength to the point where he could no longer make effective decisions.[46]

SCHWERPUNKT — THE WITHDRAWAL OF 5 BRIGADE
WEDNESDAY 21 MAY
TO FRIDAY 23 MAY 1941

What a night & what a day . . . How my heart aches.

— Sergeant James W.G. Pickett 1475, near Galatas, 21 May 1941[1]

As dawn broke on 21 May a single aircraft landed on the beach near the Tavronitis river mouth, bringing ammunition and returning to Greece with the wounded General Meindl. Another landed on Maleme airfield, but was hit by artillery fire from 27 Battery. Soon afterwards the drone of transports resounded over the airfield, and once again the sky over Maleme filled with parachutists.

Overnight, Student had taken the 'grave decision' to commit his remaining paratroops to Maleme, the first step in a bold plan to make the airfield the decisive pivot — the 'schwerpunkt' — of the battle. From Student's perspective it was a gamble. His forces had made progress around Maleme, but were no more than 'very tired remnants' of the once-proud Assault Regiment. Student feared that a concerted New Zealand attack — even as late as the morning of the 21st — would wipe out his men.[2]

The first priority was fresh ammunition and reinforcements. He had a few companies of paratroopers left, and issued orders for them to join the Assault Regiment. Part of 5 Mountain Division had been due to fly to Heraklion. Now he ordered them to Maleme as soon as the airfield was available. The pilots were instructed to crashland if necessary.[3]

Student also ordered the No. 1 Motor Sailing Flotilla to embark. This was part of a

Two New Zealand soldiers stand near German parachutes after the attack.

DA470 Kippenberger Military Archive & Research Library, Army Museum, Waiouru

fleet of 63 fishing boats, coasters and barges that Admiral Karlgeorg Schuster had sent to Milos, 80 miles north of Crete. Although slow, all were ideally suited to coming in close to the shore in shallow waters, or entering the small port at Canea. Schuster had obtained Italian support to the extent of two destroyers and a dozen smaller warships, and they had apparently been meant to reach Crete on 20 May, but were evidently delayed because the Italian government would not permit its warships to sail when British warships were in the vicinity. [4]

Twenty-five of the makeshift transports, known generally as the 'Light ships unit Maleme', and escorted by the destroyer *Lupo*, finally left Milos at 10 a.m. on 21 May. They had embarked heavy weapons, supplies, part of a mountain battalion and part of 2 AA Regiment. However, reports of British warships in the area — euphemistically referred to as 'the sea situation' in the official German report — prompted Schuster to order them back to harbour.

They sailed again at noon, but their miserable speed of four knots, coupled with the sea conditions, meant they did not arrive off Crete until about 10 p.m. that night. [5] 100 Mountain Regiment were ordered to embark on the second amphibious wave.

The 5th Mountain Division arrives
Wednesday 21 May

Old Bernie [Freyberg] was delighted with his battle and was watching Maleme with the greatest interest — as was I, but saying to myself (as one did day after day when things got worse and worse) this IS the end.

— J.K. Elliott[6]

Oberfeldweber F. Teichmann of the Meindl Sturm (Assault) Regiment was among the 350-odd paratroops dropped west of Maleme on the morning of 21 May, supported by forces from six Ju 52s that came in on the beach. He left Megara aerodrome 'having been told by the OC of their Coy that they would not meet with much opposition'. W.G. McClymont interviewed Teichmann after the war and was told that the Germans:

. . . left their planes some 3 km west of the aerodrome and dropped to some flat ground near the sea coast . . . After landing they footed it very quickly towards the Tavronitis river and the houses just west of the river. Some used the motor cycles which had been dropped with them. There were also trucks from the aerodrome which the Germans were using. In Holland they had learned how to drive captured British vehicles. There was some artillery fire while they were re-grouping.

They were organised very quickly and told by one officer who had landed in the first wave

(20 May) that 'this was no exercise'. Then, an hour or so after landing they left quickly to join in the battle for there were few parachutists in the area. Crossing the bridge over the Tavronitis river they were shot at by rifle fire and 5 or 6 parachutists were killed or wounded. These shots came from one solitary NZ sergeant who . . . when asked why he fought alone when everybody else had gone replied that it was sport for him to do that . . . They [the Germans] were amazed . . .[7]

The Germans intended to advance far enough to silence the New Zealand artillery batteries, which would let the Mountain Division fly into the airfield. The advance was planned for the afternoon, originally around the coast, but:

. . . there was fire from houses on the aerodrome so they [the Germans] did not cross the road but went along it and . . . to the south of it. They met with heavy fire from the ridges due east, particularly from . . . Point 107 . . . and artillery shells were landing on the aerodrome. The day was spent on the ridges south of the 'drome.[8]

From the New Zealand perspective a counter-attack seemed urgent by mid-afternoon, but Hargest believed German air superiority and an absence of strong artillery support would delay the manoeuvre until after nightfall. That afternoon Freyberg conferred with Puttick, Inglis and the Australian commanders, during which messages arrived confirming that the amphibious forces were on their way. This prevented him releasing 1 Welch Battalion from Canea to stiffen the counter-attack. Puttick was reluctant to strip 4 Brigade of more than a battalion as a result of the strong German lodgement south of Galatas. He was able to obtain only two infantry battalions — 28 (Maori) and 20 — backed by several light tanks from 3 Hussars and artillery of the 2/3 Royal Australian Regiment. Even then, the 20th was not permitted to move from the coast near Canea until relieved by 2/7 Australian Regiment, coming up from Georgeoupolis.

During the afternoon several houses north of Pirgos fell into German hands. About 2.30 p.m. the air attacks over Maleme rose to a crescendo and the Assault Regiment advanced towards Pirgos. By this time the New Zealand line had been reinforced by C Company, and the Kiwis broke up the attack. Student's last para-troopers — 5 and 6 Companies of II Parachute Regiment — now came down northeast of Maleme, between Pirgos and Platanias. They met a hot reception from 19 Battalion and elements of 28 Battalion. [9]

Despite artillery fire the Germans worked very hard to get the airfield operational through the day, even using prisoners of war

to clear wrecked aircraft and debris. Around 3.30 p.m. the Ju 52/3ms began bringing the Mountain Division into Maleme, landing amid ongoing artillery fire from the New Zealanders. Captain Baker of 28 Battalion D Company had taken two platoons to deal with an enemy-occupied house, and saw a 'huge concentration of troop carrying planes'. [10] Elliott saw the Junkers arrive 'with the regularity of trains' every two minutes.

Maleme even at our distance was the best imitation of inferno that I ever want to see . . . We could count about seven or eight crash landed planes on the beach — some of these were burning. The aerodrome was covered with crashed and burning planes. It was obscured at intervals by dust and smoke. It was being shelled quite heavily by our guns and we could see them getting direct hits on planes as they landed . . . In spite of all this the big German planes were coming down steadily and landing in the smoke and explosions. [11]

At least twenty aircraft were destroyed on the ground by Kiwi artillery fire — but not before their valuable troops and cargo had been discharged. The Germans tried clearing the wrecks with a captured tank, and diverted later aircraft to the beach. Constant attack by the Luftwaffe hampered Kiwi efforts to intervene and by the end of the day nearly 800 men had been landed.

Puttick reached divisional headquarters

Gordon Round
(centre), Jack Jenkin
(right) and a fellow
soldier on Crete.

with orders for the counter-attack around 7 p.m. A conference at 5 Brigade HQ about an hour later was attended by Hargest, 28 (Maori) Battalion Commander Lieutenant Colonel G. Dittmer, and Divisional GSO, Lieutenant Colonel W.G. Gentry. The start was fixed for 1 a.m. next morning, about the time of an expected RAF air-raid, and the moment when 20 Battalion was expected to arrive from the outskirts of Canea. The main objectives were the airfield and the Tavronitis bridge. Hargest added 23 Battalion to the assault force and ordered 28 Battalion to withdraw to its original coastal position near Platanias once it had achieved its objective.

By this time the invasion flotilla was not far north of Crete. Freyberg sent a message to Puttick 'warning of the likelyhood [sic] of an enemy landing from the sea during the night or at dawn'.[12] Puttick told Inglis at 9.50 p.m. that 'early sea borne attack in area CANEA likely', advising him of efforts to stiffen 'existing defences' from the Kladiso river to Khalepa. As part of the defensive effort Inglis was put on notice to move 4 Brigade at short notice, with support from an Australian machine-gun battalion. This essentially killed any chance of 20 Battalion being released from its coastal position before it was relieved.[13]

Naval action north of Crete

Stick it out. Navy must not let Army down. It is essential no seaborne enemy force land in Crete.

— Admiral Sir Andrew Cunningham, Commander in Chief Mediterranean Fleet, to his commanders, 22 May 1941 [14]

The waters north of Crete were completely dominated by the Luftwaffe and very hazardous for ships without air cover. Daylight operations were almost impossible, and Admiral Cunningham ordered his forces to enter the area only at dusk on both 20 and 21 May. [15] If the first amphibious invasion force had been able to make the crossing successfully during the day on 20 May, as planned, there would have been little the Navy could have done to stop them. Indeed, the same was true of the next day.

However, because of head winds the Germans were still at sea when cruiser forces under Rear Admiral I.G. Glennie and Rear Admiral E.L.S King advanced into the waters north of Crete late on 21 May. [16] For some hours the Germans seemed to have slipped the net, but around 11.30 p.m. Glennie's cruiser force finally intercepted the 25-strong 'Light ships unit Maleme', just over twelve miles north of Canea. [17] Glennie's ships quickly overwhelmed the *Lupo*, and 'in a scrambling engagement in the dark' devastated the transports. [18] The two-and-a-half-hour action was visible from the shore and watched by many troops, including Freyberg and his staff at CREFORCE. [19]

Harold Loftus had a grandstand view and watched 'the navy destroy Hitler's convoy . . . Heavy guns far away & tracers & shells & flaming onions close at hand.' [20] J.N. Kinder, whose unit was on its way from Galatas to reinforce the artillery batteries around Maleme, heard of 'a big landing by sea which was being attempted', and:

. . . as there was no hope of getting through to the guns that night we were put up on the hill to keep watch. The Maoris had gone on a charge right through to the aerodrome . . . We occupied their look out positions and for the rest of the night witnessed an amazing sight. Out at sea the navy were engaging the German ships and the sight of tracer shells streaming through the dark in a steady stream was one never to be forgotten. Flares sent up made it look like a glorious Xmas, but it meant different to the 16,000 enemy troops [sic] who never reached the island. [21]

The seaborne invasion relied on a makeshift flotilla of caiques. Here, Germans load their gear at Chalkis ready for the voyage to Milos and then Crete. The comprehensive range of field equipment issued to each soldier is clear from the packs in the foreground. The bipod-mounted MG-42 machine guns at bottom right were standard issue, and remained in service when the German Army was reformed after the war.

DA11992 Kippenberger Military Archive & Research Library, Army Museum, Waiouru

The Germans suffered 'considerable' losses,[22] mostly equipment — their casualties were only slightly over 300[23] — and the only invaders to reach Crete from this invasion force were what Peter McIntyre called a 'small boatload of half-crazed German soldiers' who drifted ashore a few days later.[24] But in the darkness and confusion on the night of 21 May this was not obvious, and one apparently reliable report arrived at Divisional HQ in the early hours of the morning, warning that Germans were landing on the beaches near the hospital. 'Numbers unknown but witness claims to have seen 50–60 rafts or boats, he could not say which.'[25] The message was phoned through to 5 Brigade at around 0500 hours — just when Hargest was waiting for first reports back from the counter-attack.

More naval action followed the next day. Cunningham's orders for the night of 21/22 May were explicit: if the full German invasion fleet was not located at night, the cruisers were to zig-zag north during the day to find it, regardless of the risk.[26] King's force sank a caique near Heraklion at 8.30 a.m., then boldly advanced towards Milos.

The German response to these developments was swift and decisive. General Freiherr von Richthofen had 228 level bombers, 205 Ju 87 Stukas, 114 Me 110 fighters and 119 Me 109's at his disposal, and by 5.30 a.m. on 22 May the Germans were searching for British units around Crete. They found and attacked the cruisers HMS *Fiji* and HMS *Gloucester*, which were hastening to join Rear Admiral Rawling's battleships south of Crete. Then they turned their attention to the waters between Crete and Milos.

Fighting through repeated air attacks, King's ships ran into several Italian destroyers escorting caiques near Milos at around 10.30 a.m. on 22 May. The RAF had identified this as the second invasion fleet, but King was behind in the intelligence loop and a smokescreen prevented him seeing exactly what he faced. As he was short on anti-aircraft ammunition, he ordered his force to withdraw.

Cunningham felt the decision was 'a faulty one',[27] but King's arrival nevertheless prompted the German convoy to scatter and return to Greece.[28] While pulling back the British force was 'bombed continuously' for three and a half hours, and the Luftwaffe attacked other British ships west of the Kithera channel.[29]

From the British perspective the Luftwaffe seemed ubiquitous, but an official report by Luftflotte IV noted that: 'During these engagements it became clear that the units of Fleigerkorps VIII were not sufficiently strong to fulfil all the tasks allotted to them.' Reinforcements were called in from other units in Greece, mainly II KG (bombers) and I/St G.1 (Stukas).[30] Cunningham nevertheless ordered that the 'night patrol to the northward of Crete' had to be maintained.[31]

Counter-attack at Maleme
Thursday 22 May

The counter-attack was scheduled to begin
at 1 a.m. on 22 May, but the Australians
relieving 20 Battalion were delayed on the
road from Georgeoupolis by air attack.
Although the naval battle was clearly visible
from the coast, the gun-flashes and flares
gave little real indication as to how it was
progressing — there were even reports of
landings — and Puttick did not change the
orders. The battalion was relieved at around
1 a.m. Major J.T. Burrows, commanding,

reached 5 Brigade HQ at 2.15 a.m., and C
and D companies got to their start point
about half an hour later. The other three
companies were still strung down the road
to Platanias, so Burrows ordered the attack
to proceed with C and D companies alone.
Hargest felt this eviscerated assault was
unlikely to succeed, and 'rang Div HQ and
asked must the attack go on. "It must" was
the reply and on it went.'[32]

At 3.30 a.m., two companies of 20

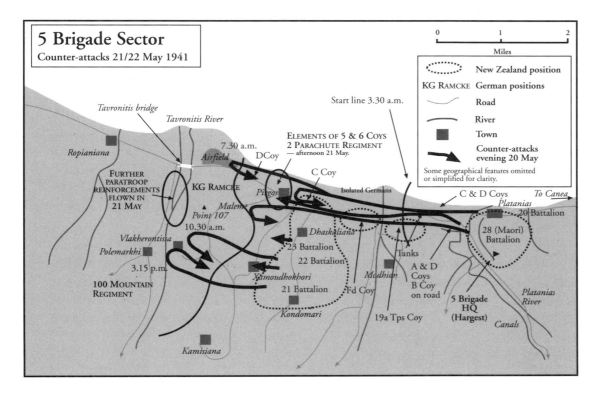

Battalion and two of 28 Battalion backed by three tanks began the advance. They quickly ran into German groups on the road to Pirgos. Some were taken by surprise, caught literally without boots or trousers in their bivouacs, but others reacted swiftly and there were heavy casualties on both sides. As a result the Kiwis did not reach the crossroads to Dhaskaliana until after dawn.

As the three New Zealand tanks approached Pirgos they were engaged by a German anti-tank battery in the town. A spirited duel followed, during which one of the German guns was knocked out, but the Germans damaged the lead tank and forced it to withdraw. The second drove into a bamboo patch to avoid air attack, where it broke down, and the third was ordered back as it was too dangerous to advance alone. Meanwhile 28 Battalion C Company entered Pirgos and immediately bogged down in ferocious house-to-house battles.

While this went on, D company — now followed by B company, which had caught up — advanced towards Maleme into heavy machine-gun and mortar fire. By the time they reached the outskirts of the airfield it was clear a full-scale German counter-attack was under way, bolstered by fresh troops spilling from arriving transports and plunging straight into action. Casualties swiftly mounted.

Lieutenant P.V. Maxwell, the only surviving officer, pulled the men into cover.

Orders then came to join 28 (Maori) Battalion in an attempt to reach the high ground above the airfield — the notorious Point 107.

The Maori Battalion advanced against bitter opposition to the stream beyond Pirgos, but there 'seemed to be German machine guns behind all the trees'[33] and progress was impossible. It was early afternoon before 20 Battalion arrived, just in time to help 23 Battalion hold the flank against a determined attack. Developing German opposition finally forced the Maori to withdraw, pulling back behind Pirgos. Further south, 21 Battalion A Company recaptured Xamoudhokhori by 10 a.m., but met heavy opposition while advancing to the high ground beyond. Some of the men made it to the ridge over the Tavronitis, but by about 3.30 p.m. steady German pressure forced the New Zealanders back.

The counter-attack spoiled a German breakthrough offensive, but it did not dislodge them. J.N. Kinder was 'pretty certain that had they started a bit earlier they would have captured the aerodrome'.[34] The real question is whether, in the longer run, success at Maleme would have made a difference. The New Zealanders might have retaken the airfield, but holding it under conditions of enemy air superiority against forces so strongly lodged to the west was another matter.

Retreat to Galatas
Thursday 22 May to Friday 23 May

I regret that it is impossible to land reinforcements at Suda Bay at present. Your gallant troops must stick at it.

— GENERAL WAVELL TO GENERAL FREYBERG, 22 MAY 1941[35]

The only significant action for the New Zealanders outside Maleme during 22 May was in Prison Valley, where Kippenberger organised an attack by two companies to retake ground lost the day before. This began around 3 p.m. but met heavy opposition, and around 7 p.m. the Germans launched a counter-attack towards Galatas. Kippenberger called up the Composite Battalion reserve, then led Lieutenant

Carson's company around Wheat Hill. They received unexpected assistance from 'about a hundred Greeks and villagers including women and children', led by Captain Forrester. The Germans broke and ran.[36]

During the afternoon Freyberg asked Wavell for further reinforcements — he had been promised 2 Battalion of the Queen's Royal Regiment — but was told it had become too dangerous to send them to Tymbaki or Suda. The best Wavell could offer was a single commando unit and the prospect of strafing attacks by fighters early next day. These would then have to land in open ground 'within your protection'.[37]

At around 5 p.m. Freyberg ordered an

Wrecked transports were strewn about Maleme airfield by 22 May. The size of this 'miserable aerodrome' is evident from this vertical shot.

DA2059 Kippenberger Military Archive & Research Library, Army Museum, Waiouru

attack on Maleme with elements of 4 Brigade, but the order was cancelled when news came of movements by the Germans against Galatas. Action against the airfield was limited to artillery fire, though this was intense. From the hill above Maleme, J.N. Kinder saw:

. . . fully 50 planes littered on the drome itself and all along the beach. Planes were still landing while incessant artillery fire kept a pall of dust over the drome. Their attack was certainly costing the enemy heavy losses all day he stayed there, although we had to keep pretty low on account of the Me 109's which were continually machine gunning the area . . .[38]

Despite the artillery fire, the Germans were able to bring in 'a further 2 battalions of 5 Mountain Div and the Mountain Pioneer Bn'. It required considerable effort; the 'landing strip, littered with burning and broken down aircraft, was cleared again and again with the help of captured tanks by a landing commando . . . commanded by Major Snowadzki'.[39]

A new threat developed against the coast road. Peter McIntyre was on his way to 5 Brigade when his truck came under fire from German snipers near Ay Marina. He reached Hargest's headquarters just before dusk, and was welcomed with a cup of tea. All was not well. 'In spite of Jimmy Hargest's pleasantness,' he later wrote, 'one could sense the strain in the dugout.' An air raid developed, forcing the men to 'stuff handkerchiefs into their mouths to relieve the frightful concussion of the bombs'. In the middle of it all the phone rang. Hargest took the call, which McIntyre assumed was from Puttick or Freyberg. 'I can't ask my men to do it,' McIntyre heard the Brigadier say. 'They've had more than enough.'[40]

The caller was actually Puttick, exploring the notion of a second counter-attack. Hargest's reaction swung the divisional commander towards withdrawing 5 Brigade to a shorter defensive line. He conferred with Brigadier K.L. Stewart and concluded that 5 Brigade would have to fall back along the coast to the Platanias River, where they would form a single line with 10 Brigade. The preparatory order was given around 10.30 p.m. and — as communications with 5 Brigade had broken down — a motorcyclist was sent about two hours later with detailed instructions.

The cost of war. German corpses amid olive groves.

No reference, Kippenberger Military Archive & Research Library, Army Museum, Waiouru

There were few opportunities to rest once the battle began; the men had to snatch every moment they could before the next wave of the relentless assault.

Part of 5 Destroyer Flotilla entered Canea bay late in the evening, attacking two caiques and briefly bombarding Maleme. Two other destroyers picked up King George of Greece from the south coast, much to Freyberg's relief — he was 'out of touch and most anxious about the safety of both parties'.[41] Many warships were critically low on anti-aircraft ammunition, and Cunningham ordered the force back to Alexandria.[42] Even so, the Luftwaffe sunk the destroyers HMS *Kelly* and HMS *Kashmir* the next day.

Freyberg renewed his demands for air support in a lengthy message to Wavell in the early hours of 23 May. The Germans had:

. . . continued to land troop carriers, not only on the aerodrome under our shellfire but also on the beaches and a strip to the west, in the most methodical way. In all, fifty nine landed between 1 p.m. and 4 p.m. today . . . to deny Maleme aerodrome to the enemy meant holding a long and vulnerable area . . . I have decided to readjust the present insecure position and make ready for a secure defence . . . The enemy is approaching equality in numbers. We shall continue to fight here and at other points in Crete . . . Our approximate line runs northwest and southeast 200 yards west of Galatas. I consider that RAF help, especially fighters, may alter the outlook and it is for very deep consideration whether this help can be made available and maintained for the next few days, which are critical.[43]

GALATAS — BATTLE IN THE BALANCE

FRIDAY 23 MAY TO TUESDAY 27 MAY 1941

The situation at Maleme is really serious.
Send all available air help.

— GENERAL FREYBERG TO GENERAL WAVELL,
23 MAY 1941[1]

General Student wanted to direct the combat personally once the troops were established, but was prevented from flying to Maleme by Goering. Instead, 52-year-old Major General Julius Ringel took over direct command, arriving at Maleme in the early evening of 22 May and reorganising available forces into three groups, named — like all ad hoc German units — after their commanders. Kampfgruppe (KG) Schaete was given the task of strengthening the positions around Maleme and moving west to Kastelli. KG Ramcke was ordered to advance east along the road, and KG Utz made a flanking assault from the south with elements of 100 and 83 Mountain Regiments.

Most of the Kiwi combat troops did not move from Maleme until after dawn on the 23rd, and the line was re-established mid-morning. Kinder's unit was 'forced to walk' due to a shortage of vehicle space, 'and thank goodness the Jerry planes were a bit later on the job that morning or they would have played havoc on the road. It was simply lined with troops . . .'[2] Dittmer was unimpressed to find that 28 (Maori) Battalion had been made rearguard, but accepted the role with stoic resignation. A party under Major H.G. Dyer was the last to move, engaging the advancing Germans with Bren-gun fire until his unit was forced back by fire from mortars and a captured Bofors.

According to Teichmann the German forces 'advanced along the coast road sector, fighting all the way and annoyed by civilians who fought fiercely. There was a priest with a long sword who had to be dealt with.'[3] Heavier opposition came when they reached

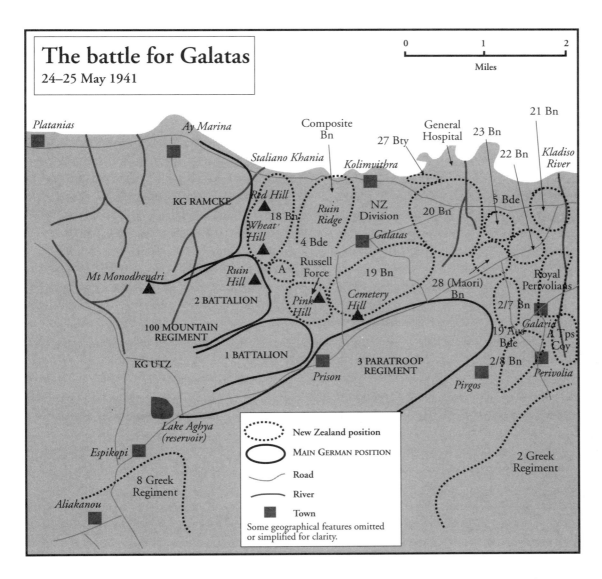

The battle for Galatas
24–25 May 1941

Platanias
Ay Marina
Staliano Khania
Composite Bn
Kolimvithra
27 Bty
General Hospital
23 Bn
21 Bn
22 Bn
Kladiso River
KG RAMCKE
Red Hill
18 Bn
Ruin Ridge
NZ Division
20 Bn
5 Bde
Wheat Hill
4 Bde
Galatas
Mt Monodhendri
Ruin Hill
A
Russell Force
19 Bn
Royal Perivolians
2 BATTALION
Pink Hill
Cemetery Hill
28 (Maori) Bn
2/7 Bn
100 MOUNTAIN REGIMENT
Galaria
KG UTZ
1 BATTALION
19 Aus Bde
A Tps Coy
3 PARATROOP REGIMENT
2/8 Bn
Prison
Pirgos
Perivolia
Lake Aghya (reservoir)
Espikopi
2 Greek Regiment
8 Greek Regiment
Aliakanou

0   1   2
Miles

⸱⸱⸱⸱⸱ New Zealand position
◯ MAIN GERMAN POSITION
⁓ Road
— River
■ Town
Some geographical features omitted or simplified for clarity.

the bridge over the Platanias River, held by elements of 28 (Maori) Battalion D Company. An initial attempt by the Germans to bring up a mortar at around 11.30 a.m. was foiled by New Zealand artillery fire, but the Germans poured more and more forces into the area and around 3.30 p.m. a resumption of shelling alerted the Kiwis to a further assault.

At that moment a small force of Blenheim

bombers attacked Maleme airfield. They destroyed a number of German aircraft on the ground and 'greatly cheered' the New Zealanders,[4] but made little real impact. An Australian artillery troop proved more useful, driving the Germans from the bridge despite counter-battery fire. B and C Companies of 20 Battalion repelled an effort to flank them along the beach.

Nevertheless, there was a dangerous gap to the south between 5 and 10 Brigades, and as the day drew to a close it became evident that the Germans were building up forces —

A German machine-gun position on Crete.

DA12650 Kippenberger Military Archive & Research Library, Army Museum, Waiouru

KG Utz, as it happened — to exploit it. Hargest had already argued that 5 Brigade needed to pull back again, and was authorised to do so mid-afternoon. He executed the order at 10 p.m.. Transport was again in short supply — there was only one truck for the whole of 23 Battalion. Two six-inch guns at Suda fired on the German positions to help the disengagement, but had to abandon the barrage when isolated German units near Suda began dropping flares on them. Nevertheless, the entire brigade had pulled back by daylight on the 24th.

The German flanking manoeuvre was hampered by terrain. 'Enormous demands have to be made on the mountain troops in this struggle,' their war diarist noted, continuing:

They are days of heavy heat. The comfortless, bare hill slopes lie defenceless in the red-hot sun. In uniforms wet with sweat the cool of the night becomes so tender. The troops do not lug even their machine guns over the trackless mountain country, and not the heavy infantry weapons, nor the mountain guns. Pack animals and transport have been left on the mainland. Substitutes are found on the island only in the tiniest quantities. The mountain paths end mostly after short ascents. Then one goes farther without a track, upwards over the steep slopes, or in the bed of the deep-cut mountain streams which, after the melting of the snow, have long since dried up. The few water places lie in the . . . hills below in the valley. In these days there is no warm food at all. The bringing up of supplies to the far-separated companies is extraordinarily laborious. [5]

Activity elsewhere in the area that day was limited. J.N. Kinder's artillery unit pulled back to the field hospital, where they came under air attack.

I was in a slit trench by myself when a 500 lb bomb dropped about 15 yds away. By wriggling my shoulders I was able to keep my head out, but the rest of me was completely buried and I had to be dug out when the raid was over . . . That night we lay up in a ditch and managed to get a decent sleep for about six hours. [6]

Conditions in the hospital were poor. Elliott visited the men early in the battle and found that the wounded 'mostly lay quietly, there was little groaning and crying. They followed you silently with their eyes and the strained manner of cheerfulness and "you'll be all right tomorrow old chap" attitude always seemed to me too transparently silly to them. I kept finding people I knew — many whose names I did not know, but whose faces were familiar.' [7]

The Germans in Prison Valley were waiting on the advance from the west, but still able to cause trouble for the defenders of Galatas. 'Talk about nerve racking,' Pickett wrote in his diary that day from the Galatas front. 'Same as yesterday.' [8] Harold Loftus was wounded:

. . . bringing a lot of ammunition from a trench across an open hill for our gun. I didn't think about bullets, though tons must have been coming & got a shock when knocked down like a rabbit or something . . . when I tried to get up they came again, so I just lay still for a few seconds or more . . . I'd called a man to . . . get the bag of magazines even while I was half-crocked! My voice sounded miles away, it's funny now but not so at the time. I was $\frac{1}{2}$ a chain from the men, so they soon got the bag. All I could think of was: 'I'm hit. Take the ammunition for the Bren — ammunition for the Bren.' [9]

Several Hurricanes from Egypt arrived over Heraklion mid-afternoon, briefly engaged a Luftwaffe bomber force, and landed at the airfield. KG Schaete advanced west to Kastelli, which was more crucial than it seemed because of its harbour. Resistance — mostly from a small squad of New Zealanders, the remnants of the Greek 1 Regiment, and local Cretans — continued through 24 May. By next day the defenders had been driven out of the village, though they continued to hold the port facilities until the 27th.

Peter Fraser's efforts to assist

The fighting has been very fierce and we can definitely say that the much-vaunted parachutists have been heavily defeated . . . [but] the scale of air attack . . . has been much worse than anything I had visualised. It has been savage. Further, our men are very tired. Indications today are that the Germans will attempt to blast their way through using 500 pound bombs . . . I know that the men will do their best but with the lack of any air support whatsoever the result with tired troops must always be in the balance.

— GENERAL FREYBERG TO GENERAL WAVELL,
24 MAY 1941 [10]

Freyberg's messages to his superiors were assuming a steady theme by the third day of the attack. He needed air support, and he needed it now. He pushed the point to Wavell in three separate messages on 23 and 24 May.[11] But Wavell did not have much to send — everything in Africa was committed, by instruction, to the Libyan campaign. To change the focus required political pressure.

The torch was picked up by Peter Fraser, who had left New Zealand to personally intervene on behalf of his countrymen. He reached Cairo on 14 May, where one Kiwi soldier saw him 'hanging about dressed very badly and probably spending a lot of money . . . I can't imagine P.F. creating much of a sensation in London.'[12] In fact Fraser was doing everything he could to get help for the New Zealanders. On 17 May he tried to get

to Crete, but was politely turned down by Freyberg. 'Although I know he will insist,' Freyberg told Middle East Command, 'Mr. Fraser could not come here without undue risk and [I] am strongly of the opinion it would be rash to allow it.'[13] On 23 May the Admiralty asked Fraser to confirm plans to deploy the New Zealand-manned light cruiser HMS *Leander* into the Mediterranean. He was delighted, telling Nash the ship was 'essential to support our men in Crete',[14] though in the event the cruiser — then in the Indian Ocean — arrived only after withdrawal was well under way.[15]

As soon as Fraser became aware of Freyberg's pleas for air support he sent a strongly worded telegram to Churchill. Although the New Zealanders were 'fighting courageously and desperately', the odds 'seem to be accumulating', he said, and:

. . . in the name of the New Zealand government I would strongly urge that all possible additional support by air and sea be immediately provided, and especially the full air assistance that can be released from all other quarters, including the United Kingdom.[16]

This was powerful stuff from a government that usually regarded itself as subordinate,[17] but Churchill was not in a receptive mood. The battlecruiser HMS *Hood* had been sunk in the Denmark Strait that morning by the *Bismarck* and *Prinz Eugen* with the loss of more than 1400 sailors, news that left Churchill looking 'inexpressibly grim',[18] according to his biographer Martin Gilbert. Faced with the simultaneous crisis in Crete, he told Fraser he could not accept the 'implications of the final sentence of your telegram. The suggestion that we are holding back air assistance for the sake of the United Kingdom is really quite unfounded . . .'[19]

Churchill had already told the House there were no aircraft on Crete 'because they have no aerodromes', which was untrue,[20] though he may have actually meant — as he told Roosevelt — that they had 'no airfields within effective range'.[21] That was true enough. Privately he believed that the loss of even half the Mediterranean fleet was a fair price for keeping Crete, and was furious with Wavell for being unable to deliver better tank reinforcements,[22] but he did not convey this to the New Zealander.

Nor was Fraser aware of the debate among the Chiefs of Staff. Lord Portal believed Beaufighters could be sent from Britain, but wanted their secret night-fighting equipment removed, which would delay their arrival until 31 May. Fraser accepted Churchill's telegram with good grace, but may have been left with the impression that the New Zealanders had been abandoned.

Wavell did what he could. Eight Wellingtons attacked Maleme on the night of 24 May,

and Hurricanes with drop-tanks took on German positions at Heraklion. Other attacks by Wellingtons and Blenheims followed. Most of the German air operations were being conducted from Scarpanto airfield, and Cunningham sent the HMS *Formidable* with a reformed air group to attack it, to some effect.

Brewing the billy under the olive groves near Galatas, New Zealand soldiers on Crete do what they can to make themselves comfortable. Makeshift equipment, including jerry-can billies, contrasts sharply with the magnificent gear the Germans provided their own soldiers for the attack. Despite Freyberg's best efforts, the British never properly replaced the gear the Kiwis had been forced to abandon in Greece.

DA11041, DA11038
Kippenberger Military Archive & Research Library, Army Museum, Waiouru

The battle for Galatas
Saturday 24 to Sunday 25 May

Counter-attack. No sleep. Lay down at 4.20 am but too much noise. Had a talk with God and feel much better.

— Sergeant James Pickett 1475, 24 May 1941[23]

By 24 May the battle had evolved into a conventional struggle in which the superior German supply situation quickly began to tell. The New Zealanders held the high ground around Galatas, but were tired and unable to withstand much more punishment from the air. This small whitewashed village was key to Crete.

Defence rested on 18 and 19 Battalions, backed by the Composite Battalion to the north and the Australian 19 Brigade to the south, the latter under Brigadier G.A. Vasey. Further south again, 2 Greek Regiment offered some protection from a flanking attack, though they were poorly armed. Hargest's 5 Brigade, notably 28 Battalion, were in contact with the German 3 Paratroop Regiment, which was advancing along Prison Valley towards the Kladiso river. The western front rested on Wheat Hill, which was overlooked by Ruin and Red Hills — of which only the latter was held by the New Zealanders — and 18 Battalion had to defend a line some 2500 yards long.

Air attacks built up during the morning while the Germans brought up heavy weapons and mortars from Maleme.

1 Battalion of 100 Mountain Regiment settled on Ruin Hill. Around noon an exceptionally heavy air raid was thought by the New Zealanders to be the start of the attack. At about 2 p.m. the Germans probed the 18 Battalion line, followed two hours later by an artillery barrage. Then the German 1 Battalion launched a determined attack against 18 Battalion C Company on Red Hill. The Kiwis fell back, but by the time Lieutenant Colonel J.R. Gray had brought up C Company the Germans had withdrawn. There was a third probing attack just on dusk.

These manoeuvres convinced Lieutenant General Wilhelm Utz, commanding KG Utz and 100 Mountain Regiment, that full-scale attack was better left for daylight when Stuka support was available. He was some way off assembling his forces and did not know that the New Zealanders were short of all but small-arms ammunition — 4 Brigade had just 72 mortar rounds left. The line was mainly held by 400 exhausted men of 18 Battalion. Freyberg put the remaining tanks under Kippenberger's command overnight and alerted Hargest that 23 Battalion might be called on. The artillery was moved back after being:

. . . in action all day playing a sort of a game with the enemy air force. As soon as the planes were a safe distance away we fired, immediately bringing them back to look for us. All round us

they bombed, but fortune evidently favoured us as [we] *were not found. As soon as it was dark enough we moved out. As there was a shortage of room in the quads many of us were compelled to ride on the guns themselves, and they certainly were not built for comfortable riding. Down the road some quad went over the bank in the dark and had to be abandoned. For me, this was disastrous, as my own kit was on it and I lost most of my belongings . . .* [24]

The Germans were still bringing up forces on the morning of 25 May, and began the day with a 'vicious [air] raid on Canea and the surrounding country'. [25] A heavy mortar, air and machine-gun bombardment followed around Galatas — 18 Battalion D Company alone suffered nineteen casualties. Return fire swiftly depleted the ammunition. When Gray asked Kippenberger for more mortar bombs he was sent all that remained — 30 rounds. The Germans were on back slopes or tucked into gullies, where they were difficult to hit, and by early afternoon the New Zealanders were in direct contact with the enemy right down the line.

It was a desperate day. A procession of RAF bombers towards Maleme brought cheers from James Pickett. After days of intolerable strain he had found peace. 'Usual straffing [sic] and mortar barrage,' he wrote; 'I can take it now. Not scared any more. Many happies Annette.' [26] They were

his last words. He stowed the tiny diary, but within hours his position had been overrun by the Germans and Pickett lay dead.

One of the heaviest thrusts came against Wheat Hill, held by 18 Battalion D Company and Petrol Company. By 3 p.m. D Company was in dire straits, and some of the outlying positions surrendered. Gray rushed up leading twenty men, crying 'no surrender!', but could not prevail against superior German numbers. Meanwhile KG Ramcke threatened to collapse the northern flank on Red Hill. Some 140 men had been sent to Galatas that morning by Inglis, made up of the remnants of 20 Battalion, under Captain D.J. Fountaine and Lieutenant M.G. O'Callaghan. Kippenberger ordered them in. They reached Ruin Ridge despite heavy air and artillery bombardment to find the Composite Battalion on the point of collapse. Kippenberger now had no reserves to meet a fresh threat against Wheat Hill. He ran forwards to see what was happening and found a 'party of women and children huddled together like little birds'. They looked at him 'silently, with black, terrified eyes'. [27] He sent a runner to divisional headquarters for help. The Germans took Wheat Hill, but although 18 Battalion prevented another thrust reaching battalion headquarters, the unit was forced back through Galatas during the early evening. This threatened to become a rout, and Kippenberger 'walked in among them shouting "Stand for New Zealand!"' and —

Freyberg's forces had few tanks on Crete, and most succumbed quickly to mechanical breakdown or enemy gunfire. For all that, Lieutenant Farran's tank made a difference during the bitter fighting for Galatas — along with the cold steel of the New Zealand infantry. This is one of the sixteen Vickers light tanks delivered to Crete a fortnight before the invasion.

DA12645 Kippenberger Military Archive & Research Library, Army Museum, Waiouru

by his colourful account — 'everything else I could think of.'[28] Help finally arrived in the form of 23 Battalion, stabilising the northern part of the front.

The battle to the south devolved to a struggle for Pink Hill, held by Russell's force. After a heavy dive-bombing attack around 4 p.m. Russell deployed his reserves. The northern slope was held by Petrol Company; but the withdrawal of 18 Battalion left them exposed. A runner sent to retrieve them was wounded — and by the time their plight was discovered they were virtually surrounded. They pulled back past Galatas in the hope of finding a defensive line to link with.

German forces advancing to take Galatas came under short-range fire from Australian artillery until night halted the engagement. Russell Force was in danger of being cut off, but four tanks arrived around 8 p.m. and Kippenberger sent two under Lieutenant Farran into Galatas. The tanks were heavily engaged when 23 Battalion C and D companies arrived. Kippenberger thought the men 'looked tired, but fit to fight and resolute'. He concluded that the time to patch the line had passed; 'obviously we must hit or everything would crumble away'. He ordered the companies to retake Galatas with the help of the tanks.[29] Fresh troops of 23 Battalion were joined by elements of 18 Battalion under Gray, and the attack began as dusk fell, led by Farran's tank. His vehicle was knocked out in the town square, whereupon the men fixed bayonets and charged. Once again cold steel prevailed over automatic weaponry. One soldier saw 'desperate panic in front of us' and realised the Germans had been caught 'in the act of forming up'. Had the charge been delayed even minutes, 'the position could easily have been reversed . . . The Hun seemed in full flight. From doors, windows and roofs they swarmed wildly, falling over one another to clear our relentless line.'[30]

The town was back in New Zealand hands as darkness fell, though flanked by German forces on both sides. Inglis hoped to use 28 (Maori) Battalion to follow up with a counter-attack, and Puttick sent Gentry to consult with the brigade commander. Gentry arrived at 4 Brigade HQ — a hole in the ground covered by a tarpaulin — to find Inglis sounding Dittmer out about the counter-attack. They concluded that to expend the last fresh unit would leave the Kiwis unable to hold the line next day; there seemed no practical way of keeping their tenuous hold on Galatas, and they decided to establish a fresh line further back. Around 10 p.m. Hargest scribbled a message to Puttick on 'Church Army' letter-head paper, advising that:

The position is obviously serious but Inglis is hopeful of [forming] a line. The Aust line on left may be intact. — The mending of the telephone line is urgent & we have men out to this end.[31]

Puttick signalled Force HQ at 11 p.m. that he was 'endeavouring to form a new line' but that 'reports indicate men (or many of them) badly shaken by severe air attacks and TM fire. Am afraid will lose our guns through lack of Tpt.'[32] Freyberg was not surprised, telling Puttick that the battalions were 'very weak and the areas they were given were too large' but that 'on the shorter line you should be able to hold them . . . You must hold them on that line and counter-attack if any of it should go. It is imperative that he should not break through.'[33] In fact men were already pulling back. In the early hours of 26 May, Gray tried to contact either 4 Brigade HQ or Puttick. He returned some hours later and, as Captain E. Batty recalled:

. . . said that we were to move back east-wards. I'm not sure that he mentioned Stylos. We moved off some time later in small groups. The sky was full of enemy aircraft and just after we crossed a small shallow stream below Canea — I remember that there were stepping stones where we crossed — one of the 18 Bn groups was attacked by two Me-110s while it was crossing an open space between olive groves. This is where Capt Lyon (18 Bn) was killed. Another man — a sergeant — had both his legs cut off just below the knee while he was lying on the ground by MG fire from one of the fighters.[34]

Withdrawal to 42nd Street

The Germans were very admiring of the way the New Zealanders had 'tenaciously defended' the hills. On the morning after being pushed out of Galatas, Ringel formed a new battle group from the 85 Mountain Regiment to 'push through in the direction of Suda Bay' while KG Ramcke continued the advance on Canea.[35] The latter advanced along the coast road towards 21 Battalion on 26 May and 'gained ground rapidly', penetrating as far as the 7 Field Hospital — 'contrary to order'.[36]

Further south the 85 Mountain Regiment was hampered by 'roadless and waterless mountains', by heat which reduced their advance to a crawl, and by 'an attack of our

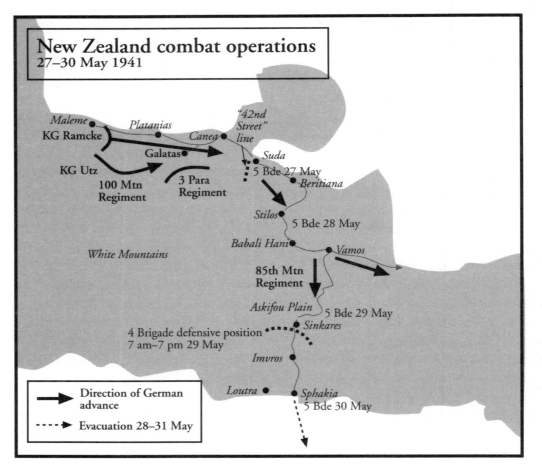

own bomber forces'.[37] Nevertheless, they advanced to Karatsos and the front line established by the New Zealanders during the early hours of the morning. Here they ran into 19 and 28 (Maori) Battalions. Although they did not deploy for full-scale assault until afternoon, when the sun was at a better angle, their probing attacks still pressed the New Zealanders.

At Pirgos, 2/7 and 2/8 Australian Battalions came under pressure from 1 Parachute Regiment, which broke through between the Australian positions and 2 Greek Regiment. The Greek commander General Achilles Scoulas told Freyberg that 'the position of the Greek forces is so difficult that they have begun to disintegrate at many points', and that if the reinforcements Churchill had promised did not promptly arrive 'the end of the struggle in Crete is . . . near at hand'.[38]

Freyberg moved his headquarters to the Suda Bay area, envisaging that 1 Welch, the Northumberland Hussars and 1 Rangers would come under Inglis' command and relieve 5 Brigade, stabilising the line. He faced a serious decision. The reinforcements and supplies he needed had not arrived, and many of the men had been fighting without food or respite for 36 hours. Defeat at Galatas led him to conclude that evacuation was the only viable military option if his men were to be saved. This was no demoralised admission of defeat. He was certainly prepared to continue, telling

Wavell that: 'If, in view of the whole Middle East position, you decide that hours help, we will carry on.' But he believed that doing so would sacrifice the men; his troops at Suda had 'reached the limit of endurance'. The military position was 'hopeless', and the men could only be extricated 'provided a decision is reached at once . . . Suda Bay may be under fire within twenty four hours . . . our casualties have been very heavy and we have lost the majority of our immobile guns.'[39] Wavell protested, so Freyberg hammered the military realities in his next message, including a coded reference:

It is obvious that you do not realise the position here. Retimo is practically foodless and without ammunition and is cut off by road in every direction . . . We can only survive provided food is landed at SPHAKIA at once . . . There is no possibility of our existing as a fighting force unless supported by adequate air. Under present conditions RBTSMOK courts disaster. Our only chance with present force which has been battered and shaken by an ovewhelming Air Force is to hide by day and to return by night to selected beaches. Once we are engaged in battle we are easy prey for dive bombers . . . I therefore urge only course is to go to SPHAKIA, which seems to give some chance of saving some of my forces.[40]

As the German assault wore on, Puttick decided that the New Zealand Division could not hold the line it had been given. He walked to CREFORCE HQ to argue the case, arriving at around 3.15 p.m. However, Freyberg needed the line held until the marine commando unit expected at Suda had disembarked. Puttick now came under the command of Major General C.E. Weston, commanding officer of the Suda area forces.

By 5 p.m. the situation on the left flank of 5 Brigade had become critical. Both Hargest and Vasey asked to withdraw. Puttick argued the case with Weston, who decided to refer back to Freyberg, but did not actually see him until well into the night. For tactical reasons Freyberg wanted 5 Brigade to hold until the Northumberland Hussars and other forces could come up from Canea to relieve them, but Weston did not get this message to Puttick.

In the absence of orders, but with a desperate situation developing, Puttick wrote to Weston:

DUKE urgently awaits your orders. Cannot wait any longer as Bde comds represents situation on their front as most urgent. Propose retiring with or without orders by 1130 hrs 26 May to line north and south through Khrystos 1553.[41]

Puttick probably meant 11.30 p.m., or 2330 hours — the original of this message in the War Diary included a marginal annotation '11.30 p.m.', which matches the time he

actually moved. The intended destination was a road running between Khristos and Tsikalaria as far as Ay Marina, nicknamed 42nd Street because the 42nd Field Company had been stationed there. It offered some protection against a breach of the left flank, and protected Suda from direct assault.

Puttick issued the orders at 10.30 p.m. on the 26th and sent Bell to advise Weston. Bell located Weston's headquarters near 42nd Street, where he found Weston asleep. At around 1.30 a.m. Puttick and Gentry decided to see Weston themselves, and while on their way to his headquarters intercepted a despatch rider carrying the orders that the New Zealand forces were to be relieved by 1 Welch, Northumberland Hussars and 1 Rangers. The two officers reached Weston's headquarters, also finding the general asleep. A brief conversation followed during which Weston agreed to Puttick's initiatives, and sent the two New Zealanders to confer with Freyberg.

The reinforcements Freyberg expected — a commando unit known as Layforce after its commander, Colonel R.E. Laycock — arrived at Suda on board the fast minelayer HMS *Abdiel* and destroyers HMS *Hero* and HMS *Nizam*. They had been delayed by the Luftwaffe. Freyberg wanted them to cover the withdrawal of the allied forces to Sphakia. The battle was over, and all that remained was the endgame.

ENDGAME — 42ND STREET TO SPHAKIA

TUESDAY 27 MAY TO SATURDAY 31 MAY 1941

Things were a bit awkward, for the Jerries had broken through a flank, but the Maoris just turned round, made a terrific bayonet charge, mopped up and chased the Jerries back nearly two miles, then calmly went on their way. The amazing thing is that they had already marched six miles over hills & through grape vines. And to think that, in the last war, those boys were formed into a Pioneer Battalion, a Labour corp [sic], because their fighting qualities were doubted!

— J.E.J. Westbrook, 17 June 1941[1]

The fortunes of war hung heavily on the mind of Winston Churchill during the gloomy night hours of 26–27 May. The *Bismarck* continued to elude his battleships in the storm-tossed Atlantic — though there were hopes she would be engaged in the morning — and two thousand miles eastward the fate of Crete seemed sealed. Defeat in either theatre was unthinkable, and at 1.35 a.m. he telegraphed Freyberg: 'Your glorious defence commands admiration in every land . . . All aid in our power is being sent.' Twenty-five minutes later he signalled Wavell that victory in Crete was 'essential at this turning point in the war'.[2] This was classic Churchillian rhetoric, but he was well aware of the realities, and when he met the War Cabinet at 10.30 a.m. had to admit that 'all chances of winning the battle in Crete now appeared to have gone'. He feared the loss of the men and, despite his promises of less than twelve hours earlier to Freyberg, admitted there was nothing Britain could do about it.[3]

By late morning the *Bismarck* had been sunk,[4] but although Churchill assured the House that the 'stubborn defence of Crete' would 'always rank high in the military and naval annals of the British Empire',[5] the prognosis remained dismal.

Bayonet charge at 42nd Street

Inglis had been unable to take command of the force reserve during the night of 26/27 May, which Weston preferred to keep under his own thumb. This group was brought up as planned west of Canea, but they were not informed of the withdrawal of 19 and 5 Brigades. Their flank — 1 Welch D Company — was consequently exposed south of Platanos. This became evident around dawn on the 27th when patrols were sent south to find the Royal Perivolians but could not locate them. They came under attack first from aircraft, then from mortar fire. Around noon Lieutenant Colonel Duncan decided he had no option but to withdraw southeast to Suda. The road was already cut, but 1 Welch B and D Companies, along with 1 Rangers, fought their way through in small parties. A and C Companies were completely cut off, and although they continued to resist into the next day they were finally taken prisoner. KG Ramcke entered Canea, while the 100 Mountain Regiment moved southeast to Suda.

By the pre-dawn hours of 27 May 5 New Zealand and 19 Australian Brigades had essentially withdrawn to 42nd Street. Not all the men were able to remain with their units. J.N. Kinder had been sent to Canea the day before, finding the town 'well smashed up and the streets . . . literally running in wine from the big store houses

. . . the streets were a mass of ruins and telephone wires and we were pretty glad to get out of the place and into our new position about a mile out of the town'. When he woke next morning he found:

. . . guns and vehicles all gone, and Jerry voices could be heard across a bit of a creek. There was Bert Teddy, Doug Jelly, Fred Grainger and myself, and the way we got out of there was a credit to Jesse Owens. We could see the marks of the vehicles and it's a wonder we were not run over. We certainly must have slept soundly. We were in a proper quandary as to what had happened so decided that the best thing we could do was to make for Suda Bay and try to find out what had happened. Down through the fields we got an indication by the quantities of war material that were left littered all over the place. Just before the bay we came to some of the other troops, but no one seemed to know just what was happening. [6]

At 42nd Street itself there was also some confusion. Vasey, Hargest and Gentry personally reconnoitred the defensive positions, but there was little they could do in the dark, and 28 (Maori) Battalion believed it was in a rear position whereas it was actually at the front. Nobody knew where the headquarters units had got to, and to cap it off, Weston did not inspire the New

Zealanders with confidence. Dittmer and Lieutenant Colonel Allen ran into him at around 8 a.m. while they were looking for brigade headquarters. Neither knew who the officer in the raincoat was. He asked them where Brigade HQ was, told them they were 'fools to stay where they were', and walked off to the northeast. Dittmer was so astonished that neither he nor Allen thought of asking who he was.[7] It is possible, as Davin has argued, that Weston believed Layforce 'A' Battalion and other troops in Suda would handle the rearguard.[8]

As water was available the New Zealanders were told to drink what they could and to wash their clothes. Ammunition was redistributed, and most of the Kiwis of 5 Brigade were enjoying a welcome respite from more than 36 hours of continuous action when the lines were suddenly spattered with automatic weapons fire. This came from 141 Mountain Regiment of Colonel Jais, which had been ordered to cut the coast road betwen Suda and Canea and was advancing in open formation without knowing that the Anzacs had established a fresh front.

The Germans ran into 2/7 Australian Battalion, who returned the fire. Further south the New Zealanders fixed bayonets and — led by the Maori — advanced steadily towards the advancing Germans, firing their rifles and sub-machine guns as they went. Dittmer ordered A and B Companies of 28 (Maori) Battalion to go,

but had trouble keeping D Company and his headquarters unit from joining the remorseless advance. The Maori pushed some 300 yards into the German lines. Further south, 19 Battalion moved forwards with D (Taranaki) Company and the Hawke's Bay contingent of C Company. The noise was phenomenal. Ray Kennedy, a stretcher-bearer with 22 Battalion, had gone to sleep in undergrowth and was 'awakened by spine tingling yells'.[9]

The number of Germans killed by the bayonet charge was never determined. Davin thought around three hundred; John McLeod suggested in 1986 that only a hundred men were actually bayoneted.[10] Either way, Jais pulled his men back in poor order and sent other units feeling out towards the coast road behind the Anzac positions. The Germans believed they had faced 'strong forces, which had only arrived on 25.5 and 26.5'.[11]

This remarkable victory by exhausted men stalled the German advance, but during the day the New Zealanders saw movement across their southern flank, suggesting they might be cut off next day. Weston could not be found, but the New Zealand commanders did locate Lieutenant-Colonel Colvin, commander of Layforce 'A' Battalion, who had been ordered by Weston to act as rearguard during the evacuation to Sphakia. This suggested that withdrawal was under way, and Hargest laid plans to move to Stylos after dark.

Behind this front the remainder of the New Zealand forces — including 4 Brigade, Divisional Headquarters and the Composite Battalion — spent the day waiting. Puttick could not locate Weston, and around 10 a.m. told Hargest:

You are technically still under Gen Weston but he cannot be located. Gen Freyberg has given you orders for tonight and tomorrow. If Gen Weston does not function Force HQ will co-ordinate future action of 5 NZ and 19 Aust Bdes. [12]

To keep the road to Sphakia open, Puttick ordered 4 Brigade to protect the approaches to Georgoupolis the following day. These

**Retreat to Stylos —
5 Brigade on the
move, 27 May. A few
were lucky enough to
ride on Bren carriers,
but most had to walk.**
DA10346 Kippenberger
Military Archive & Research
Library, Army Museum,
Waiouru

orders were confirmed by Freyberg at 4.55 p.m.[13] The Brigade moved soon after dark, followed by Divisional HQ at about 8.45 p.m., but then a message came from Hargest asking for artillery support to cover 5 Brigade disengagement, and for trucks to carry the wounded. Puttick told Hargest:

We have arranged for 4 Inf Bde to move to ASKIPLIO PLAIN for protection against airborne landings and to hold northern exit of plain where there is strong posn but 4 Inf Bde is very weak and disposed partly against parachutists . . . Major Leggitt [sic] has only 30 men and has joined 4 Inf Bde. Location remainder 4 Inf Bde unknown. All other tps moving through here have been ordered direct to Spakia [sic] . . . establishing our HQ close to southern exit ASKIPLIO plain. [14]

This plain was a plateau in the White Mountains, linked to northern Crete by a narrow, unsealed, winding road. The New Zealanders had been dropped off the command chain as a result of losing contact with Weston, but the whole day was characterised by command paralysis. Freyberg could not authorise evacuation without Wavell's approval; Wavell could do nothing until he heard from his own superiors. Finally, at 3.50 p.m., he issued the order on his own authority. A message from London saying essentially the same thing arrived three and a half hours later.

Stylos and Babali Hani
Wednesday 28 May

My position is now serious. We hold line yesterday subjected to heavy bombing and heavy ground attack which we repulsed. Extricated ourselves last night arrived here before dawn . . . No other troops except 19 Aust Bde are of any use to us. We will endeavour to hold small position here today and move back tonight but owing to exhausted state of tps this will be very difficult. We will do our damndest but look to you to give us all the assistance you can. We would still like you to send up the guns.

— Brigadier Hargest to Brigadier Puttick, 28 May 1941[15]

If the Germans had pursued the retreating forces with full vigour, it is unlikely the evacuation could have been as successful as it was. However, General Ringel was abysmally served by aerial reconnaissance and unaware of the direction of retreat. During the early hours of the 27th he decided 'to continue the encirclement of Chania [sic]' and to move 'strong forces' south of the town 'to gain the line Neon–Chorion–Stylos–Megkorafia, and be able from here to launch the pursuit towards Rethimon [Retimo]'.[16] He was determined to relieve the German forces at Retimo and Heraklion, and most of his forces pushed east while the Allied troops slipped away south, followed mainly by elements of the German 100 and 85 Mountain Regiments.

By the dawn hours of 28 May, 5 Brigade had successfully withdrawn to Stylos, but they had barely stopped before part of the 85 Mountain Regiment topped a ridge less than 400 yards away. Two companies of 23 Battalion rushed to engage. Ferocious hand-to-hand fighting followed, and the battle spread to include nearby elements of Layforce. Hargest's original plan had been to rest during the day, but the situation prompted him to order a risky daylight withdrawal to Vrises, at the feet of the White Mountains. He coordinated with adjacent Australian battalions and established his own headquarters in Babali Hani. By this time part of 3 Battalion of the 85 Mountain Regiment had begun to advance in the direction of the New Zealanders, but came up against Layforce D Battalion, deployed near the Babali Hani crossroads to protect the New Zealand rear. They successfully delayed the German advance with the help of the Australian 2/8 Battalion.

The narrow road over the mountains was jammed with men and vehicles when 4 Battalion and the remains of the Composite Battalion reached it on the night of 27 May. Transport was scarce; vehicles that ran out of petrol could not be refuelled, and others broke down or crashed off the narrow winding road in the darkness. Some vehicles were pushed into the valley below to clear

ABOVE: With a rattle and a roll, a broken-down truck goes over the edge during the climb over the White Mountains. This was the only way the narrow and crowded road could be kept open — and it also put the vehicles out of reach of the Germans.
DA12183 Kippenberger Military Archive & Research Library, Army Museum, Waiouru

RIGHT: Staff Sergeant T.C.J. Reese (1905–68) fills his water bottle with muddy liquid from a disused well during the arduous climb over the White Mountains. His face reveals the intense strain of battle. By this time the men had been fighting continuously for days, often without food, snatching sleep when they could.
DA8185 Kippenberger Military Archive & Research Library, Army Museum, Waiouru

the road. There was little clean water. Wells were dirty and polluted, though still used by thirsty soldiers. Trucks and other vehicles rattled through the formations of marching men.

For most it was a nightmare fifteen-mile ascent through rugged terrain. The officers led by example. Kippenberger, reeling with fatigue, marched at the head of 20 Battalion. Lieutenant Colonel Gray of 18 Battalion walked up and down his own lines, berating the men and herding stragglers. Half-hour advances were punctuated by five-minute pauses. The Composite Battalion reached the top at 2.30 a.m. on 28 May, after a seven-and-a-half-hour climb. J.N. Kinder crossed at the same time, finding the road:

. . . a mass of troops and vehicles with the wounded and in the dark walking was a nightmare. By 4 a.m. on the 28th we were near the top of the pass and stopped for a rest in some rocks. We stayed here all morning resting and then off we moved again and by *next morning arrived at the village where they were attempting to collect the troops into groups ready for embarkation.*[17]

Freyberg crossed in a commandeered car with a leaky radiator which ended up being pushed by a truck. Most of the transport was reserved for the seriously injured. Some men regained contact with their units during the climb, but many did not. Kinder and a small party had decided to head for Suda Bay, but:

. . . no one seemed to know just what was happening. There was a lot of talk about evacuation so we went . . . right up on the hills away from the road. This was lined with troops but we had no wish to provide a target for the Luftwaffe so kept well away from it, although the walking was very hard. By mid afternoon we had covered the first several miles and came to an Aussie food dump, where we were able to gather a few tins of beans. Most of the food had already been taken and we just had to eat what we could get. Just as we moved out enemy planes were reported and then I had about the most uncomfortable time I should like to remember. Cover was pretty scarce, and I was forced to hide in a depression no more than six inches deep and the way I bored down into that cavity was a credit to a mole or any ground dweller. For the next two hours we thought all hell was let loose as in addition to the bullets which were flying round a fire was started in a

patch of grapes just across a bit of a ditch, and we were in danger of getting well singed. At last the planes moved off home and we lost no time in getting on the road. We were told that the assembly place was some 28 miles away and orders were to move at night as much as possible.[18]

The road entered the mountains at a pass overhung by a rocky promontory, which overzealous Royal Engineers blew up just as Hargest led his battalion and Australian units towards the climb on the night of the 28th. They had to abandon their few vehicles and make a long detour on foot around the rubble, a 'long agony of broken stones' according to Hargest.[19] Exhausted men who had not eaten for days dropped out, desperate to rest, before staggering on with the general press of people. At the top, 23 Battalion moved into a defensive position. The only unit to come through in reasonably good order was 28 (Maori) Battalion, which marched into the Askifou Plain in high spirits. Men continued to pour into the plain during the day and were organised into groups, although Kinder found:

The size of the groups varied considerably according to the ideas of the officer who was collecting the men, but 50 was the most common figure. We were then sent away from the road to wait for evening when we were to move off again. In the evening we came down

Two views of the cave above Sphakia which, by 28 May, had become CREFORCE headquarters.

Sir John White Collection

to find the officer in charge of our group gone . . . We attached ourselves to another group and were told that we might not get away that night but would move nearer the beach in readiness for next night. We had about 7 or 8 miles to go and it took us almost all night to do it. First thing in the morning we again crept into the rocks and for the second time our officer left us as soon as we were asleep. After these brave actions we decided to trust to our wits and so moved down the hill to near Sparkia [sic] where all the troops were gathered in a deep rocky gulch waiting for word to embark and here we found members of our own Rgt., so put in our names with them for embarkation. [20]

A brief respite. Inside the headquarters cave at Sphakia, General Freyberg's batman helps him pour a gin and lime juice. To his right sits Captain Morse, Chief Naval Officer, Crete.

Sir John White Collection

The way down to Sphakia from the cave.

Sir John White Collection

Evacuation
Wednesday 28 to Friday 30 May

By 28 May, Admiral Cunningham's sailors were 'on the verge of complete exhaustion, physically and mentally', and his ships had 'been driven hard for more than two months' without proper maintenance. Nevertheless, he believed the 'Army could not be left to its fate. The Navy had to carry on.'[21] Privately he told one of his staff that it took the Navy three years to build a ship, but 'three hundred years to rebuild a tradition'.[22] He planned to take 1000 men from Sphakia on the 28th, 6000 on the 29th, and 3000 each night on the 30th and 31st May. Freyberg ordered a series of delaying actions, ordering 4 Brigade to hold a position on the Askifou plain during the 29th; they withdrew while a fresh force of marines held the south exit of the plain during the following day.

Freyberg's immediate problem was getting the evacuation order to the beleaguered garrisons of Retimo and Heraklion. As he had moved his headquarters to Sphakia, he was 'not yet in touch by wireless with Retimo' and 'not certain of being able to establish wireless communication', but in any case they did not have cyphers. Freyberg was reduced to asking Wavell to have a message dropped alerting the Australian garrison to the pull-out, presaged by a coded radio signal to say it was coming.[23] Units at Heraklion were told to be ready for evacuation 'about midnight'.[24] Two light cruisers and six destroyers arrived around 11.30 p.m. on the 28th to take the 4200 men. Departure was delayed when the destroyer HMS *Imperial* broke down following bomb damage, as a result of which the force was still near Crete and heavily pounded by air attack the next day. One disastrous hit on the cruiser *Orion* killed 260 men and wounded another 280.[25]

Evacuation from Sphakia took some days. Four destroyers deposited rations and took about 230 walking wounded and 800 other men from Sphakia on the night of the 28th. More men were brought south to the beach as those already there were taken off. There was a very real risk that the Germans might surge forwards, over-running the men gathering on the Askifou plain and strung out down the road to the beach, but at first the Germans seemed reluctant to advance. Gentry, writing to his wife, remarked that the 'temporary lull' was 'hard to understand but is not difficult to appreciate & I am sitting in a sunny hillside with a reasonable chance of being evacuated tomorrow evening if all goes well. A couple of days ago I did not really expect to have that chance I must confess.'[26]

Food was very short. Kinder 'heard on our arrival that supplies had been landed but had just been finished so we just tucked in our belts another inch. Our last meal had been at the Aussie dump so we were pretty hungry but there was nothing we could do so we just lay down and waited for our turn to go to the boats.'[27] Tom Castles fell in with a party from 28 (Maori) Battalion, where 'we had to make up a party of 50 to get off Crete'. Meanwhile, 'to keep the tucker up . . . [the] boys had shot a donkey up the hillside but when they went to skin it they couldn't get near it for Jerry mortar fire . . . we all built our hopes up of getting off Crete that night, but each night was the same reply "no more tonight".'[28] There were rumours that men were drawing lots, though J.N. Kinder 'never saw any and to my knowledge you were just lucky or unlucky'.[29]

The wounded were embarked first. Harold Loftus, one of the walking wounded:

Walked every night for 4 nights till daylight, hungry & thirsty. Hiding all day, with planes over us with devilish persistence. Well then, the last march of us wounded, along a rocky beach & hill road, from 9 p.m. till 1 a.m., when we were put on wonderful big boats that dropped the end down into shallow water or on the sand even & let us on, over 100 at a time. Then off to the ships & on to a welcome hard to believe. Dear sailors; gallons of thick cocoa, cup after cup for it seemed hours, then rest if possible, though all that time I couldn't move my shoulder much . . .[30]

There were fears that disorder might break out. Kinder heard that: 'a crowd of Greeks had tried to rush the boats but were not successful, and were driven off'.[31] By order, part of 28 (Maori) Battalion cordoned off the evacuation beach one night, and Westbrook's unit 'formed a cordon of fixed bayonets around the beach to stop any unauthorised person from crashing in. Only a certain number from certain units were . . . embarked, the rest had to take their chances until tomorrow night'.[32]

The Germans moved forward while the evacuation went on. A series of rearguard actions kept the beach-head clear and protected the men being steadily brought south from the assembly areas. Disengaging the rearguard units while preserving the defence was tricky.

During a conference with the brigade commanders and Weston early in the afternoon of the 29th, Freyberg decided to use 4 Brigade to protect the southern exit of the Askifou plain until 11 p.m., at which point they would march to the beach. Hargest was ordered to trickle 5 Brigade back during the afternoon. By this time 23 Battalion was in sight of German advance parties at the north of the plain, and disengaged with the help of Australian 2/7 Battalion. The Germans were engaged by fifty men of 18 Battalion A Company as they crossed the plain. Despite staunch opposition they flanked the New Zealanders with a machine gun, but Inglis called down fire from a nearby Australian artillery battery, armed with three old Italian 75-mm pieces. They fired all their ammunition — 40 rounds — to instruction, knocking out the machine gun and slowing the Germans until dusk.

By this stage the remaining New Zealanders were south of the Askifou plain, strung along the road to Sphakia, many in small units. Weston took over operational control of the rearguard action. Freyberg ordered Puttick to embark the divisional HQ unit on the night of the 29th, when Cunningham planned a 'really big effort'.[33] Puttick gave his orders and went to CREFORCE HQ with Gentry. As it happened the headquarters unit lost its place in the embarkation because of stragglers piling up on the roads. Puttick was unaware of this and embarked with Gentry on schedule at 9 p.m.. Freyberg was then ordered by Wavell to return to Egypt himself 'at first opportunity', but the instruction arrived too late for him to comply that day.[34]

The force going to Sphakia for the night of the 29th — including the valuable transport *Glengyle* and the Australian cruiser HMS *Perth* — was attacked during the day on its way in. They arrived off Sphakia around 11.30 p.m. and collected some 6000 men over the next four hours. The *Glengyle* left three landing craft for later use. The convoy was attacked three times on the way back to Alexandria, and in discussion with Air Marshal Tedder and Blamey, Cunningham decided to send four destroyers for the

night of the 30th, but felt no more ships should be risked.

Final rearguard resistance north of Sphakia came during 30 May from three tanks and several Bren gun carriers near Imvros, supported by the Australian 19 Brigade and part of 21 Battalion. One of the

19 Battalion at Sphakia. For most, the wait to be evacuated was stressful.

DA10331 Kippenberger Military Archive & Research Library, Army Museum, Waiouru

Most of the men lifted from Crete were taken off by warships — vessels hardly geared for taking passengers. Naval authorities were deeply fearful of the terrible carnage that would follow a bomb hit under such crowded conditions, and indeed nearly 500 men were killed or wounded by a single bomb that struck HMS *Orion* during the evacuation of Crete.

tanks was damaged, and the remainder pulled back behind the village. The damaged tank had to be destroyed, but with the support of a unit of Royal Marines the rest held the Germans up. By about 5.30 p.m. the armoured vehicles were short of fuel and ammunition, and were destroyed by their crews, but they had done their job. Utz organised a flanking attack down the Sfakiano Ravine, only to find this covered by the Australian 2/8 Battalion. Vasey spotted a group of Germans who had come through another part of the ravine. He had sent 20 Battalion to the beach and tried to get their two rear companies to deal with the interlopers. Kippenberger saw the danger and sent A and C Companies into action. One platoon under Charles Upham worked around the clifftops, despite the danger, to bring plunging fire on the advancing Germans and end the attack. For this and earlier action at Maleme, Upham was awarded his first Victoria Cross.

Bad news came during the afternoon. Unwilling to risk losing a warship crammed with soldiers, Cunningham decided that only 250 men could be picked up by each of the four destroyers expected that night. Freyberg had already concluded he would have to leave 21 Battalion behind, and this news forced him to leave the whole of 5 Brigade with the exception of 28 (Maori) Battalion. It was a difficult decision. Inglis

was determined to get 1000 men away, and Kippenberger was particularly unhappy. Then two of the destroyers had to turn back. Freyberg told Wavell he was:

. . . *in despair about getting these British, New Zealand and Australian Imperial forces off who have fought most gallantly in the rearguard. Do your best for us. Send one last lift tomorrow night. We could embark anything up to 7000.*[35]

Wavell assured him all was being done that could be, so Freyberg turned to Fraser with a single poignant message: 'Can you get more ships to evacuate us tomorrow night?'[36] At 7 p.m. he handed command to Weston, and a few hours later Sunderland flying boats landed in the bay to collect him. Inglis had still not departed and — despite his protests — was ordered to do so by Freyberg. The aircraft took off around 11 p.m. Jack Griffiths recalled that 'there was only the General and I' on board from Freyberg's staff, as 'John White had gone already [by destroyer] with the documents and a report to General Wavell'.[37] Two destroyers arrived soon afterwards at Sphakia, and some 1400 men were embarked — more than anticipated. The last to climb aboard was Jim Seymour, who waded out to a landing craft just as the door lifted and jumped to catch the rising edge.[38]

Peter Fraser's intervention and the final sealift
Saturday 31 May to Sunday 1 June

Fraser had primed Nash to be ready for the worst as early as 27 May. 'I feel the situation in Crete has become impossible,' he telegraphed; '. . . it must be accepted that the . . . [evacuation] will be a hazardous one and that New Zealand losses are to be expected.'[39] A number of 'injured British ships of war' in the Alexandria docks were proof of the fighting around Crete.

On the 30th, in response to Freyberg's requests, Cunningham decided to risk sending four fast ships to Crete for the night of the 31st. He wanted to 'take every man that could be crowded on board' but — particularly after the calamity on board HMS *Orion* — was concerned about the 'casualties that must ensue if a ship were badly hit'.[40] During the afternoon of 30 May, Fraser was asked to sign a message informing Freyberg that no more ships could be sent after 31 May. The men left behind were to surrender. Blamey had already signed for the Australian govern-ment, and Fraser 'understood . . . that the cablegram had been agreed to by the Chiefs of Staff, Wavell, Tedder and Cunningham'. He informed Cunningham's Military Liaison Officer, General Everetts, that 'I could not possibly sign it . . . I considered that a further effort should be made and that another ship, or ships, should be sent to

Sphakia'. As a small country New Zealand would view the loss of such a proportion of its fighting force as a 'crushing disaster'.[41]

He hammered the point again in a face-to-face meeting, and Cunningham agreed to add the cruiser *Phoebe* to the final evacuation force, although she had yet to return to Alexandria after picking men up on the night of 29 May. When she arrived at around 11 p.m. on the 30th, Cunningham offered the exhausted crew a chance to be relieved, but they volunteered for the return journey, and the ship immediately turned around with the fast minelayer *Abdiel* and the destroyers *Kimberley*, *Hotspur* and *Jackal*. Freyberg reached Alexandria about four hours later and was met by Fraser. The following morning Fraser, Freyberg and Carl Berendsen — then head of the Prime Minister's Department — went to see Cunningham and persuaded him to order the *Phoebe* to pick up every man she could. 'As a result,' Fraser later reported, '. . . in spite of the General Staff decision that no more ships would be sent, over 3000 New Zealand soldiers were rescued from the Germans.'[42]

The five ships sent to Crete for the night of 31 May, and the two cruisers supporting them, represented half the operational force left to the Mediterranean fleet — reduced to

---

two battleships, three cruisers, a minelayer and nine destroyers.[43] This intervention was subject to conflicting demands from Britain. The Admiralty had already frowned on the level to which Cunningham had expended his forces rescuing the soldiers.[44] Churchill had a different idea and apparently pressured the Vice Chief of Naval Staff to get more ships sent on the night of 1 June, but by the time the First Sea Lord had passed the message on, the troops had been ordered to surrender.[45]

The men at Sphakia did not know until later of Fraser's intervention. For Hargest the 31st was a 'day of horror . . . There were hundreds of loose members, members of non-fighting units & all sorts of people about with no formation, no order of cohesion. It was a ghastly mess.'[46] Both Hargest and Weston thought about 950 New Zealanders could be embarked that night, but Weston believed the Navy would also come back on the night of 1 June and planned his defences accordingly. He still thought this was the case as late as 4 p.m., when he told Wavell that 9000 men remained.

Then the news came that only 3500 would go, and around 8 p.m. Cunningham passed on a message from Wavell, authorising the capitulation of any troops not picked up that night.[47] The men of 5 Brigade were among those selected to go, and around 9 p.m. they began marching to the beach. The five ships arrived at about midnight, and landing craft hidden around the coast began ferrying the men on board. They were followed by part of the Australian 2/7 Battalion.

Weston prepared to depart by

HMS *Nizam* returns to Alexandria on 30 May, laden with troops plucked from Sphakia. Although most of the men are lining the rails for their arrival, the sheer numbers packed on board are evident. *Nizam* had been slightly damaged by a near-miss only a few hours earlier.

DA1621 Kippenberger Military Archive & Research Library, Army Museum, Waiouru

Commander-in-Chief of the Mediterranean Fleet, Admiral Sir Andrew Browne Cunningham (centre) with New Zealand Prime Minister Peter Fraser (right), waiting to welcome troops returning from Crete.

DA1176 Kippenberger Military Archive & Research Library, Army Museum, Waiouru

Sunderland, ordering Hargest — who was loath to leave his men until more had embarked — to come with him.[48] By 2.30 a.m. the last of the soldiers had been embarked and the ships left at speed.[49] J.C. Quinlan was among those left behind. He had arrived at Sphakia with a small group on the 30th but found there was no room on the ships. Telling himself that tomorrow was another day, he found a place to sleep.

Waking early next morning I incautiously left my blanket & went looking for other RMT. Found Kingy & returned to find blanket gone also Veale, Tommy & everyone. The valley was filled with soldiery under the trees sleeping, chatting, getting water from the well & it was like a race day at Ellerslie, once you lost anyone they stayed lost. Kingy I & someone else (I forget) stayed on the hill side hungry, we heard of some onions in the village

& managed to gather some. I had a tin of bacon in my bag . . . a tin of bully so we mixed all in a tin hat & invited two Tommies in for a feed. Our emergency rations had all gone by now. Afterwards I wandered down the valley & found Clarrie looking v. tired and worn preparing to sleep. We talked for a while & then he slept & I continued my search for Tommy. I found Veale in the end & he said the 50 party business was still going Tommy would arrange it. So in the end I found him & all was fixed. We settled on the hill just above the well & at dark settled down for sleep. Very hungry everyone & disgusted with no evacuation as yet. We were still certain of setting off.

He was disappointed. Weston left command in the hands of Lieutenant Colonel Colvin, who then found Lieutenant Colonel Walker of 2/7 Australian Battalion — a superior officer — and passed on Weston's orders to surrender. Quinlan recalled that:

Everything went dead quiet. You could hear a pin drop, every man was left to his own thoughts, that's if he could think. Now and again you would hear a shot ring out further down the waddi. Some unfortunate poor chap was taking his own life.[50]

J.N. Kinder heard that 'word had been sent to the enemy that we had capitulated' and was 'filled with utter horror'.

One Aussie blew his brains out but that didn't help much and the rest of us prepared for the arrival of the enemy. Most of us were wondering whether the Jerries would feed us, as we were all getting weak with hunger and dysentery which was rife. The latter was the worst of the two and many men were by now mere skeletons. We set to work and piled our arms and equipment and then destroyed any papers which might be of use to the enemy. [51]

After some time Walker found an Austrian officer, to whom he surrendered. In their own account the Germans linked the surrender to a light gun on Height 892 which 'opened well aimed fire', whereupon:

The enemy, as a result of this fire, abandoned his positions, aimlessly sought shelter elsewhere and hoisted white flags. Thereupon all units of I and II Bn advanced to the attack, occupied the villages Komitades, Sfakia and Lutre and took prisoner some 9000 British and 800 Greeks . . . This great success of the Regt was achieved with small losses.

They grudgingly admitted that being 'cut off from all food and ammunition supplies for 3 days may have influenced . . . [the] surrender'.[52] The fact that surrender had been ordered at the end of a difficult evacuation was probably not lost on the Germans, but was not something to be admitted in an official document.

Some of the men escaped. A few took to the hills, some joining guerrilla bands. Others commandeered the *Glengyle*'s three landing craft, one of which reached Sidi Barrani on the night of 8–9 June. The other two reached Egypt on 10 and 11 June. A caique with five officers and 148 soldiers reached Mersa Matruh on 9 June, and on 29 July the submarine *Thrasher* rescued 78 soldiers who had been hiding in the hills.[53] However, the majority fell into German hands. Kinder found that the 'Jerries [were] very decent to us and seemed to show great respect for the colonial troops as fighters', but then learned that he had met Austrian alpine troops. 'We very soon learned the difference between them and the proper Germans.' The Kiwis were marched to the village,

. . . where we were searched for arms, knives etc and then collected in the trees to wait . . . I could not help noticing that in a corner of the village a wireless had been speedily erected and the news flashed to Berlin . . . good old Major Bull of the 5th Field . . . told us . . . we would have to go back to where we had come from and they could try and feed us en route. This was better than our own army had done so we had no cause to grumble. Off we went and it wasn't long before Capt. Hardy of F Troop just collapsed and died. Half way up the hill to the road was a small grove of trees where the Jerries were busy bringing in light guns and mortars which were to have been used to blast us out of our refuge. Here one

A NEAR-RUN AFFAIR

German was sorting out some men who I suppose looked better than the rest and I was one. They took us over, sat us down and then gave us a tin of our own bully between two and a packet of biscuits each. This was all right but then I saw some of our boys coming in loaded down with enemy equipment, so as soon as some of them turned their backs I was off and rejoined the men leaving up the hill.

They were marched the long, weary way

The long march into captivity. Men ordered to surrender at Sphakia found themselves having to march all the way back over the mountains again, this time with only the prospect of a prison camp ahead. Prisoners met streams of German traffic moving to Sphakia.

DA12646 Kippenberger Military Archive & Research Library, Army Museum, Waiouru

back across the island, a tough call on men already exhausted, hungry and injured.

As long as we kept moving the guards did not bother us and I understand that those were their orders. We arrived at our first halt . . . and here were all herded into an open patch of fields where we spent the night. There was no food here but we were told that we would be fed on the road next day. We were off again by 8 a.m. and made the journey over the pass before the sun got too hot. About 2 p.m. we were down on the flat and here we were issued with a tin of bully to 4 men and packet of biscuits . . . there was a bit of a stream, and I was soon into it. My feet were well blistered, but the wash did them good and I only wish I had had some clean socks . . . By night we had arrived at the Aussie PID where I had been machine gunned on the way over and here we camped again. This was merely a repetition of the night before and in the morning we were off on our last leg.[54]

Near Canea the men were herded into the old hospital site, where — as Tom Castles recalled — they 'stayed . . . for a few weeks then they shipped us to Salonika where they herded us into the old Turkish barracks and fed us on horse soup'.[55] Despite the prospect of captivity, most of the men were relieved just to stop. 'Thank God my march was over,' Kinder wrote. For 11,835 New Zealand, Australian and British soldiers the prison camps of Germany lay ahead.

Return to Egypt
Saturday 31 May to Sunday 1 June

Good old Navy. They have saved our bacon twice now at very serious risk to themselves.

— LIEUTENANT COLONEL W.G. GENTRY TO HIS WIFE, 2 JUNE 1941 [56]

The troops lifted from the beach were not quite out of the woods as they sailed for Alexandria. Lieutenant Colonel William Gentry's ship suffered '7 lots of bombings on the way over . . . It took about 24 hours to get here & I slept & ate my way through most of that period. It was sheer bliss to eat fairly decent food again & a bit of NZ butter was better than any ambrosia. We all overate.' [57] Westbrook was given 'a packet of woodbines and a feed of stew, bread, jam and tea' after arriving. 'The crew treated us real fine,' he wrote a few days later.

They were all after souvenirs such as Lugers, German tommy guns, etc. . . . Had a shower and a shave, the first since the start of the blitz, then tried to sleep on the floor . . . At ---- we were attacked by Jerry dive bombers, two near misses making the ship buck around a little . . . A movie camera was there and a YMCA reception committee who gave us 2 bars chocolate, 20 cigs, pkt biscuits, orange, tooth brush and paste, soap and hot cup of tea. Shortly afterwards we embussed on trucks for ---- [Cairo] where we were issued with a complete messing outfit & given a dinner of hot stew, spuds, bread, butter & tea. The YMCA were on hand again and gave us more chocolate, cigs, soap, shaving soap & razor blades. Were shown to a tent and turned in for a decent night's sleep. This goes to show where the NZ Patriotic funds are used. I reckon it has been the first time we have really benefitted by it. The following day we were given more free stuff + free shaves + haircuts as well. [58]

Gentry and Puttick were met at the dock by friends who took them to the Windsor Hotel where they 'tasted the delights of bacon and eggs again. Selwyn & I did a bit of shopping & then . . . a bath. I couldn't remember exactly when I bathed last though I did have one during the month in Crete, also of course numerous sponge downs.' Gentry had lost all his equipment and 'rather enjoyed a lot of shopping. This time I am really destitute and so are we all . . . Everything has had to be thrown away . . . I am going to have to buy a lot of stuff again.' [59]

Fraser went to the docks to welcome the last contingent, finding them 'all in great heart, whether wounded or fit'. [60] He still had hopes that some of the remaining New Zealanders might yet be brought off, and nothing but praise for Cunningham, who had taken 'the greatest risks' to help, even

A NEAR-RUN AFFAIR

RIGHT: **Rescued troops disembark in Alexandria at the end of May.**

DA8172 Kippenberger Military Archive & Research Library, Army Museum, Waiouru

FAR RIGHT: **Safe at last in Alexandria, a soldier displays his booty from Crete — an MP-38 or MP-40 9 mm sub-machine gun. The weapon is missing both stock and magazine. The MP-38 and MP-40 could fire up to 500 rounds per minute, and were virtually identical, the only difference being that the latter was optimised for mass production. More than one million were made during the war. It was used with devastating effect on Crete, but many MP-38/40s nevertheless fell into New Zealand hands.**

DA1624 Kippenberger Military Archive & Research Library, Army Museum, Waiouru

'on one occasion, ignored an Admiralty order in an attempt to rescue our men'.[61] Hargest too hoped that more could be done to rescue the men, meeting Fraser as soon as he got back to argue the point, but he was told 'all had been done that could be'.[62] Nash broke the news to the people of New Zealand next day.

The men were given seven days' survivors' leave. Gentry found he could get compensation for his loss of kit 'so that side

of it won't be so bad . . . My only new asset is an excellent German torch which has been most useful.' He watched *Gone with the Wind*. 'It is just a week since our good ship touched the welcome shore of Alexandria,' he wrote to his wife on 7 June:

I have loafed most of that week though I did shift to Helwan the day before yesterday & sat in an office again . . . Yesterday all those from Crete who are not on leave paraded for Mr

Fraser & did the usual march past etc. He spoke well again. In the afternoon he threw a party to the troops at Maadi club at which they were regaled with an enormous tea. [63]

Fraser visited the wounded soldiers and 'shook hands with all that had been to Crete'. Harold Loftus 'gave him my left hand. He seemed glad to hear about things if anyone spoke. Some chaps teased him of course.'[64] For most of the men the return came as a relief, and some found new strength within themselves. Loftus was surprised at:

. . . the way my nerves acted in what is considered danger; they never once let me down & the old heart seemed to just keep its old beat, though I'd get a queer feeling when bombs were hurtling to earth 4 or 6 at a time with their screaming noise like a note of Hell: & sweat would come too if lying in sun for ½ an hour . . .

He also did not regard himself as anyone special:

I've done some talk about myself maybe, but it's about hundreds of braver men than I, as they were sick men, lots of them — heroes, lame, shaken by bombs etc. . . . I was able to walk good as ever, though when it was over I did get lazy & wonder how one could do it & get no rest in the day, 'cos of planes. No-one can sleep when planes are going round in great circles, as one never knows what each new airman might do, & I'm no hero really, just an ordinary fellow. [65]

Ray Kennedy felt that although his unit had been in London during the blitz and was later 'chased out of Greece', it was 'the terrible Battle of Crete that sorted out the men from the boys. It was our unit's first real battle and every second man became a casualty.'[66]

The perspective of history

Losses during the battle for Crete were substantial. Some 1800 Anzacs, British and Greek soldiers were killed, and nearly 12,000 captured — more than a third of the combat soldiers on the island. New Zealand lost 597 men killed. A further 136 died of wounds, ten died on active service during the campaign, one man was still listed missing as late as 1949, and 1039 were wounded; 2205 were prisoners of war, of whom 496 were wounded and 31 later died of their wounds in prison.[67]

The Mediterranean Fleet, which had put up such a magnificent performance in support of the army, was virtually gutted. Cunningham felt 'very heavy hearted'[68] at the loss of 1828 men along with many of the operational warships. Three cruisers and six destroyers were sunk, and thirteen other ships had to be withdrawn for extensive repairs.

Churchill claimed that they had inflicted 15,000 casualties on the Germans.[69] Officially some 3714 Germans were killed or listed as missing, and 2494 wounded — more than they had suffered during the Greek and Yugoslav campaigns — but actual numbers were probably higher.[70]

Criticism began even as the last troops were returning. Hargest had been incensed by the situation his men faced during evacuation and marched off to see Wavell almost as soon as he arrived in Egypt:

. . . dirty & unshaven with the only clothes I possessed not having been removed for twelve days, I pushed my way to the Embassy & told General Wavell & Admiral Cunningham the truth of many things without once knuckling down. Peter Fraser stood by me God Bless him & instead of being ashamed of my appearance was loyally proud.[71]

Hargest met Fraser, Berendsen and Fred Waite the next day to tell his story, confiding to his diary that 'I hope it will bear fruit.'[72]

The general defeat became a more intense issue over the next few days. Churchill told Roosevelt on 31 May that it had been 'impossible to continue the defence of this outpost without jeopardising the naval superiority in the eastern basin on which the rest of the Nile campaign depends'.[73]

However, media opinion in Britain quickly swung against the Prime Minister. The *Daily Mail* openly blamed British policymakers for not seriously fortifying Crete.[74] Churchill quickly asked to talk with a New Zealand officer who had been through the battle. Hargest was to have gone, but he came down with influenza and Inglis went in his place.[75] By 7 June Churchill was pressuring Fleet Street editors to tone down their vituperation. Three days later he made a one-and-a-half-hour speech to the Commons to answer criticism over the battle — particularly the lack of anti-aircraft guns and air power — arguing that Crete was 'only one part of a very important and complicated campaign' in the Middle East.[76] However, he had to admit that the 'decision to fight for Crete was taken with the full knowledge that air support would be at a minimum'.[77] Privately he blamed Wavell, a view reinforced when he met Inglis on 13 June and concluded that Middle East command did not have a 'real grip' on the defence of Crete.[78]

Churchill also anticipated that the victory would be 'exploited for the full of enemy propaganda'. As early as 31 May he was pressuring Roosevelt to draw attention away from the Mediterranean by garrisoning Iceland with 'even a brigade'.[79] Germany indeed lost no opportunity to milk the victory. Britain, the Nazi propaganda machine quickly declared, 'will fight to the last Australian or New Zealander'. Churchill was at pains to 'repudiate the German taunt' in the House on 10 June.[80]

German air superiority was largely blamed for the outcome. There was no doubt in Freyberg's mind that German air superiority was critical; afterwards he wrote that they had been beaten not by 'ordinary conditions', but by the 'great aerial concentration against us . . . The bombing is what has beaten us, the strafing having turned us out of position after position. Bombs of a heavy calibre from heights of about 200 feet simply blew our people out of the ground.'[81] Freyberg was not the only one to make this observation.[82] Hargest was convinced that 'the complete lack of aircraft to co-operate is rightly put down as the cause of our defeat'.[83] Churchill too seemed to understand the difficulties of operating under conditions of complete enemy air superiority, telling Roosevelt that the 'force and fury of the air attack' on Crete was 'beyond anything known or expected'.[84]

The same issue was formally raised by the New Zealand government through Commonwealth channels on 5 June, when Nash telegraphed Cranborne to explain that the government was 'most anxious to obtain a full appreciation of the question of air support in relation to the campaigns in Greece and Crete, and particularly why it was not possible to afford more adequate air support for the protection of their forces . . .'[85]

Fraser himself thought that 'all our care' to ensure that New Zealand troops would 'fight only on reasonably equal terms as far as equipment and supplies are concerned . . . has been rendered nugatory by the turn of events'. He concluded that 'with the means at Freyberg's disposal the island was in fact indefensible against the scale of attack which actually developed', and told the government that 'unless the necessary adequate air protection is available . . . in no case must we again allow our New Zealand troops to be exposed to a situation requiring them to meet a highly developed mechanised attack armed solely with their rifles and their courage'. He also explained this to the British 'as forcibly as possible'.[86] The message got through. Months later, when the British planned to use the revitalised New Zealand Division in the western desert, Churchill was at pains to assure Fraser that 'we shall have good air superiority'.[87]

Churchill ordered an official investigation at the beginning of June. The Court of Inquiry — chaired by Brigadier A.G. Salisbury-Jones — met during the third week of the month. They interviewed senior officers, notably Hargest, Andrew,[88] and Freyberg. Their final report exonerated Freyberg, and again identified the main problem as enemy air superiority. They also criticised British commanders in Cairo for giving Freyberg an impossible task. This document could have reduced much of the controversy that followed, but it was quickly suppressed by British command in Egypt — ostensibly because it threatened to expose the ULTRA secret, but in fact because of its criticism of their own performance.[89] Churchill had no doubts about the latter. He appointed Tedder as new Commander in Chief of the Middle East Air Forces, and soon afterwards found an excuse to sack Wavell. But Churchill also had doubts about Freyberg's conduct, and when he came to pen his memoirs in the late 1940s found heroes of the Crete campaign only in Cunningham and the Royal Navy.[90]

The clear opinion at the time was that air power had been the decisive factor; but this seemed to lose importance after the war when debate centred on the performance of individual commanders. Hargest received much of the blame for losing Maleme. Kippenberger thought he had been exhausted by the Greek campaign, but others were more critical. Hargest was killed in action in 1944, yet feeling against his performance in Crete was so high among some servicemen that when Dan Davin came to write the official campaign history in 1949 he was explicitly warned about it by Angus Ross.[91] Davin himself found fault with both Hargest and Andrew at Maleme. The latter was very unhappy with this verdict, suggesting to 22 Battalion historian Jim Henderson in 1955 that there would be arguments if Henderson's work did not agree with Davin's, but a 'private history I know of will also no doubt have them talking when it is finished . . . The 22nd chaps who were there know what I did in Greece and Crete. I'll abide by their judgement and I know why the alleged official history was written that way.'[92]

Until ULTRA was declassified in the mid-1970s, historians could not really get to grips with the full depth of events. By then, the focus of analysis had swung to Freyberg, and the new ULTRA material fuelled a vigorous debate that continued through the 1980s.

Laurie Barber and John Tonkin-Covell

found little wrong with Freyberg's actions in a solidly based 1989 analysis.[93] Two years later, however, British author Antony Beevor argued that Crete was lost because Freyberg misinterpreted ULTRA information, essentially that he had focused too heavily on defending against a seaborne invation.[94] Debate was further fuelled in 1997, when Saul David raised arguments similar to those of Beevor, and suggested that the New Zealanders had individually been no match for German paratroopers.[95]

A review of David's book in *New Zealand Defence Quarterly*[96] prompted vigorous responses to this suggestion from Lieutenant General Sir Leonard Thornton and the Hon. Sir John White, both of whom had served through the war with Freyberg and had direct experience of his abilities as a general, and of the fighting qualities of the New Zealanders. They also had access to extensive archival documentation in New Zealand, including the first ULTRA-derived information received by Freyberg on Crete at the end of April 1941. Thornton pointed out that the 'briefest reading of the operational reports' was sufficient to 'give the lie' to David's 'rash statement' that the Kiwis had proven no match for the Germans.[97] White — who had been with Freyberg on Crete — succinctly summarised the realities:

With the foreknowledge provided by ULTRA, General Freyberg deployed his forces to defend the airfields, the ports and the lines of communications vulnerable to attack from the air and the sea. That deployment was remarkably successful in engaging the attacking parachutists at each airfield and in the areas of the ports, but in the end it was complete German control of the air which was decisive on land and at sea. Crete was lost, but the battle gives the lie to Saul David's allegation that 'the ordinary soldiers . . . time and time again proved no match for the determined paratroopers'.[98]

This discussion came at a time of renewed public interest in New Zealand's military heritage, and even six decades after the battle it was clear that the Crete experience retained the power to prompt intense debate.[99]

The battle for Crete: a near-run affair

The bombing is what has beaten us, the strafing having turned us out of position after position. Bombs of a heavy calibre from heights of about 200 feet simply blew our people out of the ground.

— GENERAL FREYBERG TO GENERAL WAVELL,
28 MAY 1941[100]

Crete was lost mainly because Freyberg was ordered to hold an island with capable but ill-equipped troops, virtually no artillery, and a handful of obsolescent tanks — all under conditions of total enemy air superiority. He had no illusions about their chances at the time, writing in June 1941 that: 'my statements that we would repel any enemy attack, were made with the intention of raising the morale of the troops'.[101]

The fact that Freyberg's strategy successfully defeated the Germans at all landing areas except Maleme is a testament both to his outstanding capabilities as a military tactician, and to the quality and determination of the troops he led. In the face of overwhelming enemy air power, however, even the best-laid plans were hampered. German aircraft provided a means of first establishing lodgements on Crete, then of moving tactically useful numbers of troops into critical areas. When backed with bombers and fighters this was decisive. The Luftwaffe hindered movement on land and sea, provided German ground troops with lethal and omnipresent 'airborne artillery', and compounded the communications problems of the defenders. Gentry summed up the problem a few days after the battle:

At some periods we were straffed [sic] continuously without cessation for as long as 7 hours. The constant drone of planes flying over the tree tops spraying the area with M.G. was very monotonous & on me at least induced great sleepiness. The effect was that you could not move about, no walkers or runner & no cars as they were sitting shots. The telephone lines were always bombed out & communication was very difficult . . . night was the time when everything had to be done.[102]

These factors proved critical. As early as 24 May Freyberg advised Wavell that the scale of air attack was 'much worse than anything I had visualised . . . I know that the men will do their best but with the lack of any air support whatsoever the result with tired troops must always be in the balance'.[103] On 27 May he was even more explicit: 'There is no possibility of our existing as a fighting force unless supported by adequate air.'[104] It was an evaluation shared by many who fought on Crete at the time, and the official investigation in June 1941 endorsed the General's views.

ENDGAME — 42ND STREET TO SPHAKIA

This understanding provides a different light in which to view the tactical decisions made by Hargest and his commanders at Maleme on 20–22 May. Historians from Davin onwards have invariably argued that the battle for Crete could have been won if only Andrew had not abandoned Maleme; if only Hargest had effectively counter-attacked that night; or if only the counter-attack of 21–22 May had begun a few hours earlier. These points would be worthy of further debate if we wish to pursue the 'what ifs'. However, historical counter-factuals invariably devolve into increasingly unlikely chains of probability.[105] Holding or retaking Maleme during the first days would have altered the detail of the battle, but — particularly given German air superiority and the German lodgements west of the airfield — we can never be certain this would have tipped the balance. In all probability it would not. Certainly this was the view of some participants; Elliott, writing a few weeks after the battle, thought that the New Zealanders might have gained the airfield on 22 May if they had moved 20 Battalion a few hours earlier, 'but the final result would only have been delayed for a few hours'.[106] Indeed, he believed that even had British fighters been stationed on Crete, the outcome would have been the same:

Crete was within easy fighter and Stuka range of numerous German aerodromes in the Peloponnese and on Milos and Rhodes and the Dodecanese. Our cramped aerodromes would have been blasted out of existence and it would have been impossible to maintain aircraft on them. Hurricanes could get to Crete from the Western Desert but to operate over Crete they would have had to use Maleme or Heraklion — both untenable.[107]

In short, the underlying cause of defeat was simply that unopposed air power proved decisive, just as air power exponent Guilio Douhet had predicted after the First World War. Although the world was still nearly six decades away from a successful air-only campaign, it was clear even in 1941 that Freyberg had been ordered to fight a modern combined battle without the right tools to do so.[108] If anybody is to be blamed for the defeat, it is Middle East command for being unable to provide adequate air cover — a truism that Churchill certainly identified soon after the battle. On this basis, the real point about the battle for Crete is not that it was a narrow defeat for the British, but that Freyberg was able to come so close to victory despite the odds. The battle was very much a near-run affair.

New Zealand soldiers certainly proved themselves a match for the paratroopers, earning great respect from the Germans. This reputation carried into the African campaign, when Rommel openly regarded them as being 'among the elite of the British Army'.[109] From New Zealand's perspective the unsung hero remained Peter Fraser, whose personal intervention in Cairo was at the very highest level — no other Commonwealth nation sent even a minister. His efforts saved New Zealanders who would otherwise have been prisoners of war for the duration, potentially at the cost of their health and lives. It was a conceptual extension of the policies his government had initiated in 1935, and marked a break from the previous attitude to Imperial relations.[110]

The narrowness of the German victory had a wider dimension than simply the fall of Crete. Freyberg made the island very difficult for the Germans to take, and afterwards Student always regarded Crete as 'the graveyard of the German parachutists'. The Fallschirmjager were never again deployed in the assault role. Malta — astride the German supply lines to Africa — was particularly vulnerable to parachute assault, but never did suffer this fate. British supply interdiction from Malta certainly contributed to the defeat of the Afrika Korps in late 1943. As far as Hitler was concerned the whole Balkan episode was a diversion that hampered deployment of the forces he needed to break his pact with the Soviets. The Panzers did not roll across the Bug River until 22 June — several weeks late.

Delays during the campaign compounded the problem, leaving Field Marshal von Bock's forces bogged in autumn mud on the road to Moscow, and then trapped by the snows of winter, tantalisingly short of their goal.

For the New Zealanders the battles of Greece and Crete were a solid introduction to the enemy. They knew what it was like to come under air attack, to suffer artillery bombardment, and to see friends killed or wounded. They knew the Germans were not invincible warriors, but ordinary men like themselves who could be matched in combat. The Kiwis knew too that they could survive hunger, thirst and injury, and that they could push themselves to the ragged edge of endurance — not through a desire to become heroes, but simply because it had to be done. They emerged from the battle for Crete with a sense of grim realism and an understanding that war could never be glorious. It was an experience that stood them in good stead when the Second New Zealand Division, led by Lieutenant General Bernard Freyberg, was pitted against the Afrika Korps and arguably one of the greatest military tacticians of all time — the Desert Fox, Erwin Rommel.

ENDNOTES

AJHR   Appendix to the Journals of the House of
             Representatives
BGS   Brigadier General Staff
LO   Liaison Officer
NZDQ   New Zealand Defence Quartely
SSDA   Secretary of State for Dominion Affairs
2NZDWD 2 New Zealand Division War Diary

Introduction

1. General Sir Bernard Freyberg, '2nd New Zealand
   Expeditionary Force, Campaigns in Greece and
   Crete', short unofficial account prepared by the
   GOC 2NZEF for the Minister of Defence,
   AJHR, 1941, H-19a, p. 3.

Greek overture

1. *Documents I*, No. 339, Prime Minister of New
   Zealand (PM of NZ) to SSDA, 26 February
   1941.
2. This was New Zealand's only Expeditionary
   Force in the war, but gained the prefix 'Second' to
   differentiate it from the New Zealand
   Expeditionary Force raised for the First World
   War. The same differentiation applied to the
   Division within the respective forces in each war.
3. For a general summary see Peter Calvocoressi
   and Guy Wint, *Total War*, pp. 145–65; Winston
   Churchill, *The Second World War*, Vol. III, pp.
   193–269.
4. Churchill portrayed the intervention to the
   House as being 'in accordance with our Treaty
   obligations'. Charles Eade (ed.), *The Unrelenting
   Struggle — War Speeches by the Right Honorable
   Sir Winston Churchill*, p. 155; hereafter Eade,
   Speeches.

5. Tony Simpson, *Operation Mercury – The Battle
   for Crete*, 1941, p. 40.
6. Martin Gilbert, *Finest Hour, Winston S.
   Churchill 1939–1941*, p. 973. These plans were
   probably precautionary.
7. Ibid, p. 1009.
8. Ibid, p. 1025.
9. Eade, *Speeches*, p. 109.
10. Gilbert, *Finest Hour*, p. 979.
11. Simpson, *Operation Mercury*, p. 36.
12. Cited in Gilbert, *Finest Hour*, p. 989.
13. Simpson, *Operation Mercury*, pp. 51–64.
14. Calvocoressi and Wint, *Total War*, p. 155.
15. Gilbert, *Finest Hour*, p. 1024.
16. See John Charmley, *Churchill's Grand Alliance*,
    pp. 18–23.
17. Warren F. Kimball (ed.), *Churchill and Roosevelt,
    The Complete Correspondence*, Vol. 1, *Alliance
    Emerging*. Roosevelt to 'Former Naval Person', 1
    May 1941, p. 178.
18. Eade, *Speeches*, p. 108.
19. Gilbert, *Finest Hour*, p. 1025.
20. Ibid, p. 1027. See also Churchill, *The Second
    World War*, p. 91.
21. See Matthew Wright, *Kiwi Air Power*, especially
    chapter 2, for discussion of 1935–38 Labour
    government defence policies.
22. *Documents I*, No. 335. SSDA to PM of NZ, 25
    February 1941.
23. Ibid, No. 339. PM of NZ to SSDA, 26 February
    1941.
24. Ibid, No. 343. SSDA to PM of NZ, 2 March
    1941.
25. Ibid, No. 345. SSDA to PM of NZ, 7 March
    1941.

26. Ibid, No. 349. SSDA to PM of NZ, 7 March 1941.

27. The prevailing attitude was one of subservience to Britain in defence matters, irrespective of the legal status of being a 'self-governing Dominion'. For discussion of Fraser's shift of policy 1941–44 towards reliance on the United States, see Wright, *Kiwi Air Power*, pp. 22–26, 106–109; also Ian Wards 'Peter Fraser: Warrior Prime Minister' in *Peter Fraser, Master Politician*, ed. Margaret Clark. For a different perspective see also Roberto Rabel, 'Where She (Britain) Goes We Go', *NZDQ*, No. 27, Summer 1999.

28. *Documents I*, No. 353. PM of NZ to SSDA, 9 March 1941.

29. Ibid, No. 354. Prime Minister of United Kingdom to Prime Minister of New Zealand, 12 March 1941.

30. Ibid, No. 356. SSDA to PM of NZ, 14 March 1941.

31. Quoted in Churchill, *The Second World War* Vol. III, p. 144.

32. WTu, MS Papers 1453. J.N. Maclean Collection; hereafter 'Maclean papers'.

33. WTu, MS Papers 2408. Harold Loftus Collection. 1941 diary, typescript; hereafter 'Loftus papers'.

34. *Documents I*, No. 27, p. 23.

35. Paul Freyberg, *Bernard Freyberg VC — Soldier of Two Nations*, p. 96.

36. Ibid, pp. 65, 92.

37. Churchill, *The Second World War*, Vol. III, p. 242.

38. Cited in Laurie Barber and John Tonkin-Covell, *Freyberg — Churchill's Salamander*, p. 263.

39. See for example, McLeod, *Myth and Reality*, pp. 170–85; also Antony Beevor, *Crete - The Battle and the Resistance.*

40. NA, WAII/8/17. Historical Papers, Orders, etc, May 1941. 'Notes of instructions to LO' (Liaison Officer).

41. *Documents I*, No. 38. Report by the Hon. Peter Fraser on his visit to England in 1939.

42. Interview with Jack Griffiths, 17 July 1999.

43. *Documents I*, No. 341. Special Order of the Day by General Freyberg to the 2nd New Zealand Division.

44. NA, WAII/8/10. Greece, Historical Papers, Orders, etc. 'Leaving Alexandria 6 March 1941'.

45. Ibid.

46. *Documents I*, No. 357. Freyberg to PM of NZ, 6 April 1941.

47. NA, WAII/8/10. PM of NZ to SSDA, 9 March 1941.

48. *Documents I*, No. 362. PM of NZ to PM of UK, 14 April 1941.

49. NA, WAII/8/10. Draft notes from Freyberg to Fraser.

50. *Documents I*, No. 447. Fraser to Nash, 7 June 1941.

51. WTu 1453, Maclean papers. Greek narrative, part 3. Letter home, 3 April 1941.

52. Ibid.

53. Ibid. The Tukituki is a river near Maclean's home town of Havelock North.

54. WTu, MS Papers 1407. Folder 3. Lance Corporal J.E.J. Westbrook Collection. Letter home, 25 April 1941; hereafter 'Westbrook papers'.

55. WTu, MS Papers 4146. James Pickett Collection, diary. Pickett's emphasis; hereafter 'WTu, 4146, Pickett papers'.

56. NA, WAII DA52/10/10. Series I. Brigadier Hargest's diaries and letters, 8 February–25 June 1941. Letter to Mrs J. Hargest, 13 April 1941. Hereafter 'Hargest papers'.

57. WTu, 1453, Maclean papers.

58. WTu, 1407, Westbrook papers.

59. Ibid.

60. *Documents I*, No. 366. PM of UK to PM of NZ, 17 April 1941.

61. Ibid, No. 369. SSDA to PM of NZ, 20 April 1941.

ENDNOTES

62. WTu, 1453, Maclean papers.
63. Ibid.
64. WTu, MS Papers 1453. Westbrook papers. Letter home 25 April/4 May 1941.
65. WTu, MS Papers 5525-3. W.G. Gentry Collection. Letters to his wife, April 1941; hereafter 'Gentry papers'.
66. Ibid.
67. *Documents I*, No. 370. Acting PM of the Commonwealth of Australia to PM of NZ, 22 April 1941.
68. Ibid, No. 372. PM of NZ to PM of UK, 22 April 1941.
69. Ibid, No. 373. PM of UK to PM of NZ, 22 April 1941.
70. Andrew Cunningham, *A Sailor's Odyssey – The Autobiography of Admiral of the Fleet Viscount Cunningham of Hyndhope*, p. 349. The other commitment was supporting Malta.
71. WTu, 2408, Loftus papers.
72. WTu, MS Papers 4165. Folder 1. George M. Craigie Collection. 'How I got away from Greece'; hereafter 'Craigie papers'.
73. *Documents I*, No. 376. General Wavell to the Chief of the General Staff (Wellington), 26 April 1941.
74. WTu, 5525-3, Gentry papers. 29 April 1941.
75. WTu, MS Papers 3792. Renouf Collection. Letter, 21 December 1976.
76. WTu, 1453, Maclean papers.
77. WTu, 1407, Westbrook papers. Letter home, 25 April/4 May 1941.
78. WTu, 5525-3, Gentry papers. 30 April 1941.
79. WTu, 2048, Loftus papers. Diary, 28 April 1941.
80. *Documents I*, No. 385. General Freyberg to the Minister of Defence, 8 May 1941.
81. P. Freyberg, *Bernard Freyberg*, pp. 261–62.
82. Churchill, *The Second World War*, Vol. III, p. 206. This number included 'several thousand Cypriots, Palestinians, Greeks and Yugoslavs'. See also P. Freyberg, *Bernard Freyberg*, p. 260, who notes that among the New Zealand POWs were a number of reinforcements sent to Kalamata and not embarked.
83. NA, WAII/52/10/10, Hargest papers. Letter to Mrs J. Hargest, 28 April 1941.
84. Ibid. Diary, 28 April 1941.
85. WTu, 1407, Westbrook papers. Letter home 25 April/4 May 1941.
86. WTu, MS Papers 91-063. Guy W. Macpherson Collection. Letter to the Greek ambassador re: Battle of Crete in 1941.
87. Churchill, *The Second World War*, Vol. III, pp. 205–06.

The attack on Crete

1. NA, WAII/8/16, BGS File, March–May 1941. 'BGS Appreciation — German plan for attack on Crete, Force HQ', 12 May 1941.
2. *Documents I*, No. 365. SSDA to PM of NZ, 17 April 1941.
3. Ibid, No. 381. Headquarters 2NZEF (Cairo) to the PM of NZ, 1 May 1941.
4. Ibid, No. 385. Freyberg to the Minister of Defence, 8 May 1941.
5. Ibid, No. 386. Acting PM to General Freyberg, 11 May 1941.
6. WTu, 2048, Loftus papers.
7. WTu, 4165, Craigie papers.
8. Peter McIntyre, *War Artist*, p. 84.
9. WTu, 1407, Westbrook papers. Letter home, 25 April/4 May 1941.
10. WTu, MS Papers 5039-232, Operation Crete – battle report of XI Air Corps Luftwaffe: the invasion of Crete, Luftflotte report, 28 November 1941. A translation of a report issued by Luftflotte 4, hereafter 'Luftflotte 4 Report'.
11. *New Zealand Herald*, 16 January 1999.
12. B.H. Liddell-Hart, *The Rommel Papers*, p. 240.
13. WTu, 5039-232, Luftflotte 4 Report.
14. Ibid.
15. Ibid.
16. WTu, 5039-232. 'Operation Crete: XI Air Corps

Battle Report' (translation); hereafter 'Einsatz Kreta'.

17. WTu, 5039-232, Luftflotte 4 Report.
18. WTu, 5039-232, Einsatz Kreta.
19. Noted by Hon. Sir John White in interview, July 1999; also Hon. Sir John White, 'The Battle for Crete', letter to the editor, *The Dominion*, 17 February 1995.
20. WTu, 5039-232, Einsatz Kreta.
21. Noted in Barber and Tonkin-Covell, *Freyberg*, p. 10.
22. NA, WAII/8/14. Crete cables Mideast 'No. 54141', 29 April 1941.
23. NA, WAII/8/17. 'Should We Hold Crete?', 28 April 1941.
24. Ibid. 'Crete. Outline of events from 20 April to 31 May 1941'.
25. *Documents I*, No. 389. Freyberg to Minister of Defence, 1 May 1941.
26. Ibid.
27. Ibid, No. 388. Freyberg to Fraser, 1 May 1941.
28. Ibid, No. 446. Freyberg to Nash, 6 June 1941.
29. Cited in Barber and Tonkin-Covell, *Freyberg*, p. 18.
30. Ibid, p. 13.
31. NA, WAII/8/14, Crete cables Mideast; also *Documents I*, No. 387. Freyberg to Wavell, 1 May 1941.
32. NA, WAII/8/14, Crete cables Mideast. Wavell to Freyberg (n.d.: early May 1941).
33. *Documents I*, No. 392. Wavell to Freyberg, 2 May 1941.
34. Cunningham, *A Sailor's Odyssey*, pp. 366–67.
35. *Documents I*, No. 388. Freyberg to Fraser, 1 May 1941. Author's italics.
36. Cited ibid, p. 13.
37. NA, WAII/8/17. 'Report on Air Operations in Crete', covering letter from Freyberg to Beamish G/35/1/DO, June 1941.
38. Cited in Barber and Tonkin-Covell, *Freyberg*, p. 15.
39. Cited in Dan Davin, *Crete*. '5 Bde Operation Instruction No. 4, 18 May 1941', p. 66.
40. Ibid, p. 17.
41. NA, WAII/DA21.1/1/17. 2NZDWD, May 1941. Training Directive G1/2 from New Zealand Division Headquarters to 5 Infantry Brigade, 20 Battalion, Russel Force, Sigs, Oakes Force.
42. NA, WAII/8/14, Crete cables Mideast. Freyberg to Churchill, 5 May 1941.
43. Churchill and Freyberg had known each other since World War I. See P. Freyberg, *Bernard Freyberg*, pp. 176–77.
44. NA, WAII/8/14, Crete cables Mideast. Freyberg to Churchill, 5 May 1941.
45. Churchill, *The Second World War*, Vol. III, p. 223.
46. NA, WAII/8/14, Crete cables Mideast. To Creforce from Middle East, 7 May 1941. He sent six heavy Matilda I tanks and fifteen light tanks.
47. P. Freyberg, *Bernard Freyberg*, pp. 273–78.
48. For example, see OL-series reprinted in Antony Beevor, *Crete – the Battle and the Resistance*, Appendix C, pp. 349–51; Barber and Tonkin-Covell, *Freyberg*, pp. 19–20.
49. Cited in Barber and Tonkin-Covell, *Freyberg*, p. 25.
50. NA, WAII/DA 21.1/1/17, 2nd NZDWD. NZ Div. Op. Instruction No. 6, 13 May 1941.
51. Barber and Tonkin-Covell argued that Dorman-Smith was taking further information to Freyberg, possibly an advance copy of OL-302. However, in light of the security procedures associated with Ultra, it is more likely Dorman-Smith had been sent to advise that information was coming. These same security precautions — which also required all secret documentation to be burnt once read — complicate reconstruction of the exact information Freyberg received during this period.
52. Cited in Barber and Tonkin-Covell, *Freyberg*,

ENDNOTES

p. 31. PRO WO 169/1334A, 'Creforce Operation Instruction No. 10', 5 May 1941.

53. NA, WAII/8/16, BGS File. 'BGS Appreciation — German Plan for attack on Crete, Force HQ, 12 May 1941'. Author's italics.

54. Argued by Barber and Tonkin-Covell, *Freyberg*, p. 19.

55. Ibid, p. 23.

56. Cited ibid, p. 34.

57. NA, WAII/8/17. 'Notes of Instructions to LO. Information for Brigadier Chappel.'

58. NA, WAII/8/14, Crete cables Mideast. To: Mideast, From: Creforce, 16 May 1941.

59. WTu, MSX 4641, Major J.K. Elliot Headquarters Division Diary; hereafter Elliott diary.

60. P. Freyberg, *Bernard Freyberg*, p. 211.

61. Barber and Tonkin-Covell, *Freyberg*, p. 20.

62. Cited in Davin, *Crete*, '5 Bde Operation Instruction No. 4, 18 May 1941', p. 66.

63. NA, WAII/52/10/10, Hargest papers. Diary, 2 May 1941.

64. Ibid. Letter to Mrs J. Hargest, 10 May 1941.

65. Barber and Tonkin-Covell, *Freyberg*, p. 30.

66. NA, WAII/52/10/10, Hargest papers. Diary, 13 May 1941.

67. Cited in Barber and Tonkin-Covell, *Freyberg*, p. 36.

68. Cited ibid, p. 35. This was the argument of Geoffrey Cox in *A Tale of Two Battles — a personal memoir of Crete and the Western Desert 1941*.

69. P. Freyberg, *Bernard Freyberg*, pp. 284–85.

70. WTu, MS Papers 5079-203. W.G. McClymont. Narrative of the Crete campaign, citing XII Air Corps War Diary.

71. Noted also by Geoffrey Cox, *A Tale of Two Battles*, p. 52.

72. *Documents I*, No. 394. Fraser to Churchill, 2 May 1941.

73. Ibid, No. 397. Nash to Freyberg, 4 May 1941.

74. Ibid, No. 396. Churchill to Fraser, 3 May 1941.

75. Ibid, No. 392. Wavell to Freyberg, 2 May 1941.

76. NA, WAII/8/17. Private letter from 'Archie' Wavell to Freyberg, 8 May 1941.

77. Ibid. 'Report on Air Operations in Crete' by Group Captain Beamish, OC (Officer Commanding) RAF Crete.

78. General Sir B. Freyberg, '2nd New Zealand Expeditionary Force', *AJHR*, 1941, H-19a, p. 3.

79. WTu, 5039-232, Einsatz Kreta.

80. NA, WAII/8/17. Freyberg to GH (General Headquarters) Middle East Forces, 10 September 1941.

81. WTu, MS Papers 5079-231. Papers relating to the Crete Campaign. Report on work and operations at Suda Bay, 17–26 May 1941, Lieutenant Colonel G.J. McNaught.

82. WTu, MSX 4641, Elliott diary.

83. WTu, MS Papers 5079-231. Papers relating to the Crete Campaign. Signal diagrams of Crete, plus Report on Signal Aspects of Campaign in Crete by Captain G.C. Pryor, 18 June 1941.

84. NA, WAII8/17, Crete cables Mideast. Freyberg to Wavell, 16 May 1941.

85. NA, WAII/8/17. 'Report on Air Operations in Crete'. Covering letter from Freyberg to Beamish, G/35/1/DO, June 1941.

86. Ibid. 'Notes of Instructions to LO. Information for Brigadier Chappel.'

87. WTu, 4146, Pickett papers. 16 May 1941.

88. Ibid. 18 May 1941.

Airborne assault

1. NA, WAII/52/10/10, Hargest papers. Letter to Mrs J. Hargest, 24 May 1941.

2. WTu, 5525-3, Gentry papers.

3. NA, WAII/52/10/10, Hargest papers. Letter to Mrs J. Hargest, 24 May 1941.

4. WTu, MS Papers 1622. Kinder Collection. Narrative; hereafter 'Kinder papers'.

5. WTu, MSC 4641, Elliott diary.

6. WTu, 5525-3, Gentry papers. Letter to his wife, 29 May 1941.

7. WTu, MS Papers 5079-231. 'Story of Oberfeldweber F. Teichmann of the Meindl Sturm Regiment, obtained by W. G. McClymont on 31 December 1945'. Hereafter 'McClymont/Teichmann'.

8. Ibid.

9. WTu, 5039-232, Einsatz Kreta.

10. WTu 1407, Westbrook papers. Letter to mother, 17 June 1941.

11. WTu, 5039-232, Einsatz Kreta.

12. WTu, MSX 4641, Elliott diary.

13. Cited in Davin, *Crete*. Gray to J.G. McLean, 24 July 1941.

14. WTu, 1407, Westbrook papers. Letter to mother, 17 June 1941.

15. Ibid.

16. Ibid.

17. Ibid.

18. NA, WAIIDA21.1/1/17 2NZDWD.

19. WTu, 5039-232, Einsatz Kreta.

20. WTu, MSX 4641,Elliott diary.

21. Eade, *Speeches*, p. 139. He corrected the error on 10 June.

22. WTu, 4146, Pickett papers, 20 May 1941.

23. WTu, 1622, Kinder papers.

24. WTu, 5039-232, Einsatz Kreta.

25. WTu, 1622, Kinder papers.

26. NA, WAII/DA21.1/1/17. 2NZDWD. Kippenberger to Headquarters New Zealand Division, 20 May 1941.

27. WTu, 1622, Kinder papers.

28. WTu, MSX 4641, Elliott diary.

29. Ibid.

30. Davin, *Crete*, p. 136.

31. Cited in Simpson, *Operation Mercury*, p. 191.

32. Wira Gardiner, *The Story of the Maori Battalion*, p. 63.

33. The MP-38 was a folding-stock sub-machine gun operating on the blow-back principle, designed by Heinrich Vollmer for Erfurter Maschinenfabrik B. Geipel GMBH (Erma), but popularly named after Hugo Schmeisser, who designed the earlier MP-28. J.B. King, *Infantry at War 1939-1945*, pp. 22–23.

34. Davin papers. Angus Ross to Davin, 4 September 1949.

35. NA, WAII/52/10/10, see notes associated with Hargest papers.

36. Davin, *Crete*, p. 137.

37. Simpson, *Operation Mercury*, p. 194.

38. *Documents I*, No. 408. Freyberg to Wavell, 20 May 1941.

39. WTu, MSX 4641, Elliott diary.

40. Davin papers. Cox to Davin 12/3/50. See also the more extended account in Cox, pp. 75–76.

41. WTu, MSX 4641, Elliott diary.

42. Hon. Sir John White, letter to the editor, *The Dominion*, 9 February 1995, original MS.

43. Davin papers. Cox to Davin, 12 March 1950.

44. Cox, *A Tale of Two Battles*, p. 74.

45. See Davin, *Crete*, p. 66.

46. See Gentry's observations on p. 112.

Schwerpunkt — the withdrawal of 5 Brigade

1. WTu, 4146, Pickett papers.

2. Student, cited in Davin, *Crete*, p. 182.

3. Noted by Geoffrey Cox, *A Tale of Two Battles*, p. 79.

4. WTu, 5039-232, Einsatz Kreta.

5. Ibid.

6. WTu, MSX 4641, Elliott diary.

7. WTU, 5079-231, McClymont/Teichmann.

8. Ibid.

9. Cited in Davin, *Crete*, p. 190.

10. Ibid, p. 189.

11. WTu, MSX 4641, Elliott diary.

12. NA, WAIIDA2101/1/17, 2NZDWD, 21 May 1941.

13. WTu, MS Papers 5079-231. Papers relating to the Crete Campaign: Selected Messages from HQ

ENDNOTES

2NZ Division 'G' Branch War Diary, May 1941.

14. Quoted in Churchill, *The Second World War*, Vol. III, p. 256; also Cunningham, *A Sailor's Odyssey*, p. 373.
15. Churchill, *The Second World War*, Vol. III, p. 286.
16. WTu, 5039-232, Luftflotte 4 report..
17. WTu, 5039-232, Einsatz Kreta.
18. Cunningham, *A Sailor's Odyssey*, p. 369.
19. Jack Griffiths, interview 17 July 1999.
20. WTu, 2048, Loftus papers.
21. WTu, 1622, Kinder papers.
22. WTu, 5039-232, Einsatz Kreta.
23. Noted by Simpson, *Operation Mercury*, p. 212.
24. McIntyre, *War Artist*, p. 64.
25. WTu, MS Papers 5079-231. Papers relating to the Crete Campaign.
26. Cunningham, *A Sailor's Odyssey*, p. 368.
27. Ibid, p. 370.
28. WTu, 5039-232, Luftflotte 4 report..
29. Cunningham, *A Sailor's Odyssey*, pp. 370–71.
30. WTu, 5039-232, Luftflotte 4 report..
31. Cunningham, *A Sailor's Odyssey*, p. 373.
32. NA, WAII/52/10/10, Hargest papers. Diary, 21 May 1941.
33. Major H.G. Dyer cited in Davin, *Crete*, p. 220.
34. WTu, 1622, Kinder papers.
35. *Documents I*, No. 414. Wavell to Freyberg, 22 May 1941.
36. Kippenberger, quoted in Davin, *Crete*, p. 234.
37. *Documents I*, No. 414. Wavell to Freyberg, 22 May 1941.
38. WTu, 1622, Kinder papers.
39. WTu, 5039-232, Einsatz Kreta.
40. McIntyre, *War Artist*, p. 81–82.
41. *Documents I*, No. 412. Freyberg to Wavell, 21 May 1941.
42. Cunningham, *A Sailor's Odyssey*, pp. 373–74.
43. *Documents I*, No. 417. Freyberg to Wavell, 23 May 1941.

Galatas — battle in the balance

1. *Documents I*, No. 416. Freyberg to Wavell, 23 May 1941.
2. WTu, 1622, Kinder papers.
3. WTu, 5079-231, McClymont/Teichmann.
4. *Documents I*, No. 418. Freyberg to Wavell, 23 May 1941.
5. WTu, MS Papers 5079-203. W.G. McClymont, narrative of the Crete campaign citing XII Army Corps War Diary; hereafter McClymont papers.
6. WTu, 1622, Kinder papers.
7. WTu, MSX 4641, Elliott diary.
8. WTu, 4146, Pickett papers, 22 May 1941.
9. WTu, 2048, Loftus papers.
10. *Documents I*, No. 423. Freyberg to Wavell, 24 May 1941.
11. Ibid. Numbers 416, 417 and 423.
12. Maclean papers, 21 May 1941.
13. NA, WAII/8/17. Creforce to Mideast, 17 May 1941.
14. *Documents I*, No. 419. Fraser to Nash, 23 May 1941.
15. Grant Howard, *The Navy in New Zealand*, p. 62.
16. *Documents I*, No. 421. Fraser to Churchill, 24 May 1941.
17. 'Subordinate' in this context meaning subordinacy of attitude as opposed to the legal position of Dominion status.
18. Gilbert, *Finest Hour*, p.1094.
19. *Documents I*, No. 422. Churchill to Fraser, 24 May 1941.
20. Eade, *Speeches*, p. 142.
21. Kimball, *Churchill and Roosevelt*. 'Personal and Secret for the President from Former Naval Person', 23 May 1941, Vol. I, p. 192.
22. Gilbert, *Finest Hour*, p. 1095.
23. WTu, 4146, Pickett papers, 24 May 1941.
24. WTu, 1622, Kinder papers.
25. WTu, 5079-203, McClymont papers. 'Narrative of the Crete Campaign', summarising official New Zealand reports.

26. WTu, 4146, Pickett papers, 25 May 1941. A German soldier picked the diary up. Via a route that included the Volksbund, the Commonwealth Graves Commission, the New Zealand High Comissioner and the Secretary of Defence, the diary came to the Alexander Turnbull Library in 1987.

27. H.K. Kippenberger, *Infantry Brigadier*, cited in Davin, *Crete*, p. 302.

28. Ibid. *Crete*, p. 303.

29. Ibid, p. 311.

30. Ibid. Lieutenant Thomas cited, p. 314.

31. NA, WAIIDA21.1/1/17, 2NZDWD.

32. Ibid.

33. Ibid, also cited in Davin, *Crete*, p. 326.

34. WTu, 5079-203, McClymont papers. 'Narrative of the Crete Campaign', report by Captain E. Batty.

35. WTu, 5039-232, Einsatz Kreta.

36. Ibid.

37. Ibid.

38. *Documents I*, No. 427. Scoulas to Freyberg, 26 May 1941.

39. Ibid, No. 428. Freyberg to Wavell, 26 May 1941.

40. NA, WAII/8/14. Crete cables Mideast. Freyberg to Wavell 27 May 1941; compare with *Documents I*, No. 429; note also coded line.

41. NA, WAIIDA21.1/1/17, 2NZDWD.

Endgame — 42nd Street to Sphakia

1. WTu, MS Papers 1407, Westbrook papers, 17 June 1941. Westbrook's reference to the use of Maori as a labour corps in World War I is not strictly true; hereafter 'Westbrook papers'.

2. Cited in Gilbert, *Finest Hour*, p. 1096.

3. Cited ibid, p. 1096.

4. Churchill, *The Second World War*, Vol. III, p. 283.

5. Eade, *Speeches*, p. 144.

6. WTu, 1622, Kinder papers.

7. Lieutenant Colonel Dittmer, cited in Davin, *Crete*, p. 375.

8. Davin, *Crete*, p. 375.

9. WTu, MS Ref. 90-305, R.G. Kennedy Collection, 'Stories about his experience as a ''Body Snatcher' during World War II'.

10. McLeod, *Myth and Reality*, p. 101.

11. WTu, 5039-232, Einsatz Kreta, 26 May 1941.

12. NA, WAII/8/14. Crete cables Mideast, Duke to Raft 0570 27 0185.

13. WTu, MS Papers 5079-231. Selected messages from 2HQ NZ Division, G-branch war diary, May 1941.

14. Ibid.

15. Ibid.

16. WTu, 5039-232, Einsatz Kreta, 27 May 1941.

17. WTu, 1622, Kinder papers.

18. Ibid.

19. NA, WAII/52/10/10, Hargest papers. Letter to Mrs J. Hargest, 31 May 1941.

20. WTu, 1622, Kinder papers.

21. Cunningham, *A Sailor's Odyssey*, p. 380.

22. Cited in Churchill, *The Second World War*, Vol. III, p. 265, also Colonel Eddy Bauer, *The History of World War II*, p. 395.

23. NA, WAII/8/14. Crete cables Mideast. Freyberg to Mideast command 067867, 28 May 1941.

24. Ibid. Freyberg to Heraklion C-in-C (Commander in Chief), 27 May 1941.

25. Cunningham, *A Sailor's Odyssey*, pp. 382–84.

26. WTu, 5525-3, Gentry papers. Letter to his wife, 29 May 1941.

27. WTu, 1622, Kinder papers.

28. WTu, MS Papers 1461, T. Castles Collection. Letter to Jim(?), 16 April 1975; hereafter 'Castles papers'.

29. WTu, 1622, Kinder papers.

30. WTu, 2048, Loftus papers.

31. WTu, 1622, Kinder papers.

32. WTu, 1407, Westbrook papers. Letter to mother, 17 June 1941.

33. Cunningham, *A Sailor's Odyssey*, p. 385.

ENDNOTES

34. *Documents I*, No. 312, n3.
35. Ibid, No. 436. Freyberg to Wavell.
36. Ibid, No. 325. Freyberg to Fraser.
37. Jack Griffiths, interview 17 July 1999. See also NA, WAII/8/17 for the list of personnel evacuated by Sunderland.
38. Jim Seymour, interview 17 July 1999.
39. *Documents I*, No. 431. Fraser to Nash, 27 May 1941.
40. Cunningham, *A Sailor's Odyssey*, p. 387.
41. *Documents I*, No. 453. Supplementary Report by the Right Honorable P. Fraser on the Evacuation of Troops from Crete, 5 October 1948. Fraser's references to 'Chiefs of Staff' and 'General Staff' appear to refer to the command in Egypt rather than the Joint Chiefs of Staff in London.
42. Ibid. The figure he quoted is not accurate.
43. Cunningham, *A Sailor's Odyssey*, p. 387. This was also the 25th anniversary of the Battle of Jutland.
44. Ibid, p. 386.
45. Ibid, p. 389.
46. NA, WAII/52/10/10, Hargest papers. Diary, 31 May 1941.
47. Cunningham, *A Sailor's Odyssey*, p. 387.
48. NA, WAII/52/10/10, Hargest papers. Diary, 31 May 1941.
49. Cunningham, *A Sailor's Odyssey*, p. 388.
50. WTu, 1461, Castles papers. Letter to Jim(?), 16 April 1975.
51. WTu, 1622, Kinder papers.
52. WTu, 5039-232, Einsatz Kreta, 1 June 1941.
53. Cunningham, *A Sailor's Odyssey*, p. 392.
54. WTu, 1622, Kinder papers.
55. WTu, 1461, Castles papers.
56. WTu, 5525-3, Gentry papers. Letter to his wife, 2 June 1941.
57. Ibid.
58. WTu, 1407, Westbrook papers. Letter to mother, 17 June 1941.
59. WTu, 5525-3, Gentry papers. Letter to his wife, 2 June 1941.
60. *Documents I*, No. 440. Fraser to Nash, 2 June 1941.
61. Ibid.
62. NA, WAII/52/10/10, Hargest papers. Diary, 1 June 1941.
63. WTu, 5525-3, Gentry papers. Letter to his wife, 7 June 1941.
64. WTu, 2048, Loftus papers.
65. Ibid.
66. WTu, 90.305, Kennedy papers.
67. *Documents I*, No. 313, n2.
68. Cunningham, *A Sailor's Odyssey*, p. 389.
69. Churchill, *The Second World War*, Vol. III, p. 268.
70. Hon. Sir John White recalled seeing extensive cemeteries on Crete after the war. Interview, 17 July 1999.
71. NA, WAII/52/10/10, Hargest papers. Letter to Mrs J. Hargest, 2 June 1941.
72. NA, WAII/52/10/10, Hargest papers. Diary, 2 May 1941.
73. Kimball, *Churchill and Roosevelt*, I, 'Personal and Secret for the President from the Former Naval Person', p. 202.
74. Quoted in Hadjipateras and Fafalios, *Crete 1941: Eyewitnessed*, pp. 220–21.
75. NA, WAII/52/10/10, Hargest papers. Diary, 3 May 1941.
76. Eade, *Speeches*, p. 151.
77. Ibid, p. 157.
78. Cited in Gilbert, *Finest Hour*, p. 1110.
79. Kimball, *Churchill and Roosevelt*, Vol. I, 'Personal and Secret for the President from Former Naval Person', p. 203.
80. Eade, *Speeches*, p. 161–2.
81. Cited in P. Freyberg, *Bernard Freyberg*. Freyberg, report to Wavell, 28 May 1941, p. 311.
82. NA, WAII/DA 21.1/1/17, 2NZDWD. Appendix O.
83. NA, WAII/52/10/10, Hargest papers. Diary, 9 June 1941.

84. Kimball, *Churchill & Roosevelt*, Vol. I, p. 202.

85. *Documents I*, No. 444. Nash to Fraser, 5 June 1941.

86. Ibid, No. 447. Fraser to Nash, 7 June 1941.

87. Cited in Gilbert, *Finest Hour*, p. 1222.

88. NA, WAII/52/10/10, Hargest papers. Diary, 20 June 1941.

89. P. Freyberg, *Finest Hour*, pp. 315–7. The report entered the public domain in 1972.

90. Churchill, *The Second World War*, Vol. III, pp. 265–69.

91. WTu, MS Papers 5079-669. Angus Ross to Dan Davin, 4 September 1949.

92. WTu, MS Papers 3953. J. Henderson Collection. Andrew to Henderson, 3 October 1955.

93. Barber and Tonkin-Covell, *Freyberg*, pp. 108–9, see also chapters 2–4.

94. Beevor, *Crete*, pp. 88–96.

95. Saul David, *Military Blunders, the How and Why of Military Failure*, pp. 333, 347–48.

96. Naylor Hillary, 'Freyberg — Unfit to Command?', book review in *NZDQ* No. 21, Winter 1998.

97. Lieutenant General Sir Leonard Thornton, KBE, CB. 'Freyberg: Fit to Fight', *NZDQ* No. 22, Spring 1998.

98. Hon. Sir John White, 'Crete — The Facts', *NZDQ* No. 23, Summer 1998.

99. Indeed, the 1990s were a period of renewed general interest in New Zealand's military history as indicated for example by article-length letter in major daily papers. For example, see 'Defence myths' by David Filer in the *Dominion*, 5 April 2000 and 'Hard lessons learned from another war' by John White in the *Dominion*, 20 April 2000.

100. Cited in P. Freyberg, *Bernard Freyberg*. Freyberg, report to Wavell, 28 May 1941, p. 311.

101. NA, WAII/8/17. 'Report on Air Operations in Crete'. Covering letter from Freyberg to Beamish, G/35/1/DO, June 1941.

102. WTu, 5525-3, Gentry papers, 29 May 1941.

103. *Documents I*, No. 423. Freyberg to Wavell, 24 May 1941.

104. NA, WAII/8/14, Crete cables Mideast. Freyberg to Wavell, 27 May 1941; compare with *Documents I*, No. 429, note also coded line.

105. Niall Ferguson (ed.), *Virtual History*, Papermac, London, 1998. Offers useful discussion of counterfactual principles, especially chapter 1. See also Eric Hobsbawm, *On History*, Abacus, London, 1998, especially chapter 4.

106. WTu, MSX 4641, Elliott papers.

107. Ibid.

108. The three-day ground campaign during the Gulf War of 1991 was secondary to the main thrust of the war, which derived from air power; NATO intervention in Yugoslavia during 1997–98 was apparently successful purely as a result of air power.

109. B.H. Liddell-Hart (ed.), *The Rommel Papers*, p. 240.

110. For the development of New Zealand wartime international relations under Fraser, see New Zealand Institute of International Affairs, *New Zealand in World Affairs*, especially chapter 2; W.D. McIntyre, 'Peter Fraser's Commonwealth: New Zealand and the Origins of the New Commonwealth in the 1940s'.

BIBLIOGRAPHY

Primary sources

Alexander Turnbull Library, National Library of New Zealand (WTu)

82-358 Twentieth Association — Papers relating to the Twentieth New Zealand Infantry Battalion Campaign in Crete.

90-305 R.G. Kennedy Collection, 'Stories about his experience as a "Body snatcher" during World War II.'

91-063 Guy W. Macpherson Collection.

MS Papers 459 B.C. Borthwick Collection.

MS Papers 1453 J.N. Maclean Collection.

MS Papers 1407 Lance Corporal J.E.J. Westbrook Collection.

MS Papers 1461 T. Castles Collection.

MS Papers 1622 Kinder Collection.

MS Papers 2408 Harold Loftus Collection.

MS Papers 3953 Henderson Collection.

MS Papers 2732 J.C. Quinlan Collection.

MS Papers 2733 J.C. Quinlan Collection.

MS Papers 2734 J.C. Quinlan Collection.

MS Papers 3792 Renouf Collection.

MS Papers 4146 James Pickett Collection.

MS Papers 4165 George M. Craigie Collection.

Davin, Daniel Marcus, 1913–1990. Literary papers: MS Papers 5039-232 Operation Crete — Battle report of XI Air Corps Luftwaffe.
MS Papers 5079-203 W.G. McClymont — narrative of the Crete campaign.
MS Papers 5079-669, 5079-231, papers relating to the Crete campaign.

MS Papers 5525-3 W.G. Gentry Collection.

MSX 4641 Major J.K. Elliott Headquarters New Zealand Division Diary.

National Archives (NA)

WAII /8/10 Greece, historical papers, orders etc.

WAII /8/14 (Series GOC NZEF/14) Crete cables Mideast (Micro 3613).

WAII /8/16 BGS File, March–May 1941 (Micro 3613).

WAII /8/17 (Series GOC2 NZEF/17) Historical papers, orders etc., May 1941 (Micro 3613).

WAII /8/43 GOC's Diary Part I, 1939–September 1941.

DA52/10/10 Series I Brigadier Hargest's Diaries and Letters, 8 February-25 June 1941.

DA21.1/1/17 2 New Zealand Division War Diary (2NZDWD), May 1941.

Interviews

Honorable Sir John White

Jack Griffiths

Jim Seymour

Private photographic collections

Honorable Sir John White

Trent Corbett

Jim Seymour

Published primary sources

Cannadine, David (ed.), *The Speeches of Winston Churchill*, Penguin, London, 1989.

Eade, Charles (ed.), *The Unrelenting Struggle — War Speeches by the Right Honorable Sir Winston Churchill*, Cassell, London, 1942.

Kimball, Warren F. (ed.), *Churchill and Roosevelt, The Complete Correspondence*, Princeton University Press, Princeton, 1984.

Kippenberger, H.K. (ed.), *Documents relating to New Zealand's participation in the Second World War 1939–45*, Volumes I–III, War History Branch, Department of Internal Affairs, Wellington 1949, 1951, 1963.

Liddell-Hart, B.H. (ed.), *The Rommel Papers*, Collins, London, 1953.

Secondary sources

Barber, Laurie and Tonkin-Covell, John, *Freyberg — Churchill's Salamander*, Century Hutchinson, London, 1989.

Bates, P.W., *Supply Company*, War History Branch, Department of Internal Affairs, Wellington, 1955.

Bauer, Col. Eddy, *The History of World War II*, Orbis, London, 1986.

Beevor, Antony, *Crete — The Battle and the Resistance*, John Murray, London, 1991.

Bennett, Geoffrey, *Naval Battles of World War II*, David McKay, 1975.

Calvocoressi, Peter and Wint, Guy, *Total War*, Penguin, London, 1972.

Charmley, John, *Churchill's Grand Alliance*, Sceptre, London, 1995.

Churchill, W.S., *The Second World War*, London, 1950.

Clark, Margaret (ed.), *Peter Fraser, Master Politician*, Dunmore Press, Palmerston North, 1998.

Cox, Geoffrey, *A Tale of Two Battles — a personal memoir of Crete and the Western Desert 1941*, William Kimber, London, 1987.

Cunningham, Andrew, *A Sailor's Odyssey — The Autobiography of Admiral of the Fleet Viscount Cunningham of Hyndhope*, Hutchinson & Co, London, 1951.

David, Saul, *Military Blunders — the How and Why of Military Failure*, Robinson, London, 1997.

Davin, D.M., *Crete*, War History Branch, Department of Internal Affairs, Wellington, 1953.

Elliott, Murray, *Vasili, The Lion of Crete*, Century Hutchinson, Auckland, 1987.

Filer, David, *Kiwis in Khaki, A Pictorial History of the New Zealand Soldier in World War II*, David Bateman, Auckland, 1991.

Freyberg, Paul, *Bernard Freyberg VC — Soldier of Two Nations*, Hodder & Stoughton, London, 1991.

Gardiner, Wira, *The Story of the Maori Battalion*, Reed Publishing (NZ) Ltd, Auckland, 1992.

Gilbert, Martin S., *Finest Hour, Winston S. Churchill 1939–1941*, William Heinemann, London, 1983.

Green, William, *Warplanes of the Third Reich*, MacDonald and Janes, London, 1970.

Hadjipateras, C.N. and Fafalios, M.S., *Crete 1941: Eyewitnessed*, Random Century, Auckland, 1991.

Henderson, Jim, *22 Battalion*, War History Branch, Department of Internal Affairs, Wellington, 1958.

Hillary, Naylor, 'Freyberg — unfit to command?' *New Zealand Defence Quarterly*, No. 21, Winter, 1998.

Howard, Grant, *The Navy in New Zealand*, Reed Publishing (NZ) Ltd, Auckland, 1981.

King, J.B., *Infantry at War 1939–1945*, Phoebus, London, n.d., circa 1970s.

McIntosh, Sir Alister, Wood, F.L.W., Boyd, Mary, Keith, Ken (eds), *New Zealand in World Affairs*, Volume 1, Price Milburn and New Zealand Institute of International Affairs, Wellington, 1977.

McIntyre, Peter, *War Artist*, A.H. & A.W. Reed, Wellington, 1981.

McLeod, John, *Myth and Reality — The New Zealand Soldier in World War II*, Heinemann Reed, Auckland, 1986.

Montgomery, Bernard, *The Memoirs of Field Marshal the Viscount Montgomery of Alamein, KC*, Collins, London, 1958.

Murphy, W.E., 'The first campaign, Greece and Crete', in *New Zealand's Heritage*, Volume 6 Part 88.

BIBLIOGRAPHY

Rabel, Roberto, 'Where She (Britain) Goes We Go', *New Zealand Defence Quarterly* No. 27, Summer 1999.

Ross, Angus, *23 Battalion*, War History Branch, Department of Internal Affairs, Wellington, 1959.

Sandford, Kenneth, *Mark of the Lion — the Story of Capt. Charles Upham, VC and Bar*, Hutchinson, London, 1962.

Simpson, Tony, *Operation Mercury — The Battle for Crete, 1941*, Hodder & Stoughton, Auckland, 1981.

Sinclair, D.W., *19 Battalion and Armoured Regiment*, War History Branch, Department of Internal Affairs, Wellington, 1954.

Taylor, Capt. R.J., *Crete — A Tribute from New Zealand*, New Zealand Army, Wellington, 1991.

Thomson, R.H., *Captive Kiwi*, Whitcombe & Tombs, Auckland, 1964.

Thornton, Lieutenant General Sir Leonard, 'Freyberg: Fit to Fight', *New Zealand Defence Quarterly* No. 22, Spring 1998.

Watt, Lawrence, 'British to blame for fiasco?', *Sunday Star-Times*, 23 May 1999.

White, J.C., 'Bernard Freyberg, VC' in *New Zealand's Heritage*, Volume 6 Part 88.

White, J.C., 'Crete — The Facts', *New Zealand Defence Quarterly* No. 23, Summer 1998.

Wright, Matthew, *Kiwi Air Power*, Reed Publishing (NZ) Ltd, Auckland, 1998.

Yeoman, Allan, *The Long Road to Freedom*, Random Century, Auckland, 1991.

INDEX

INDEX

INDEX

ABOUT THE AUTHOR

Matthew Wright is a professional historian, and the author of more than 350 feature articles and numerous books. He has degrees in history and anthropology, and wrote his MA thesis on aspects of New Zealand's naval defence policy. He has been writing for many years on subjects ranging from defence policies to colonial social history, engineering history, historical land claim issues and forest industries. He won an award in 1996 for his interpretation of New Zealand provincial history, and pursues an active interest in New Zealand's military history.